FOUR RULES OF
FIREARM SAFETY

[1]

Treat all firearms as if they are loaded.

[2]

Always keep your firearm pointed in a safe direction.

[3]

Keep your finger OFF the trigger until ready to fire
and target is in sites.

[4]

Be sure of your target, what lies around it,
and beyond it.

GUN POINTS

FIREARMS, THE SIGNATURE OF FREEDOM

GABRIEL K. CHALFA

Published by Freiling Agency, LLC.

P.O. Box 1264
Warrenton, VA 20188

www.FreilingAgency.com

PB ISBN: 979-8-9874834-1-1
eBook ISBN: 979-8-9874834-2-8

CONTENTS

INTRODUCTION

"AMERICA IS ON A GUN-BUYING SPREE," according to Rosalina Nieves and Theresa Waldrop, of CNN. They note the escalating number of FBI background checks, the indicator that's been "soaring to record highs", they say in their report of 04 June 2021. As of 2019, the firearms industry reached an annual sales figure of $63.5 billion, up more than 232 percent in a decade, with no sign of a slowdown. (Economic Impact of Gun Industry Up 232% since '08,3/18/2021 by National Shooting Sports Foundation gameand-fishmag.com)

During the month of March 2021, alone, the FBI reported 4.7 million pre-purchase background checks, the highest recorded in their 20 years of record keeping. Though 2020 was a record year for firearm sales, the first half of 2021, continued at a fierce pace as well. More than 9.8 million FBI checks, as required for firearm purchases, are on record for the period. Reports from 2022 confirm the ever increasing demand. Nearly half of these are first-time gun owners. (nssf.org/articles/numbers-don't-lie-public-safe-ty-concerns-driving gun-sales , 08/16/2021)

Undocumented immigrants, a group previously denied access, may, on occasion, possess firearms based on the Supreme Court ruling of 21 June 2019. Another recent trend is the increasing number of women arriving at sales counters and practice ranges. In a recent "Wall Street Journal" story, Zhsha Elinson reported that 3.5 million women became new gun owners from January 2019 to April 2021. (wsj,com/articles/women-are-nearly-half-of-new-gun-buyers 9/20/21).

Numerous sources report that gun sales to black women and men have increased substantially. Some buyers tell me they don't even like guns, but they are beginning "to see the need."

Without doubt, interest in firepower is high. Recent months have been fraught with increased crime, social upheaval, protests, reduced police protection, overflowing immigration, and, with the fall of Afghanistan, increasing threats of terrorism. All these events tend to leave the populace a bit edgy and concerned about victimization.

Help for emergencies has slowed. The average law enforcement response time to a 911 call is varied and dependent on factors such as phone service, dispatcher's understanding, proximity and availability of enforcers, and other variables. The situation is aggravated in this time of calls for defunding police, and the resulting degradation in their numbers. Dispatchers of some municipalities have had to put emergency calls on hold. Think about that! Why are thousands of people put on hold when they call 911? (Michelle Boudin, From wcnc.com 24 Feb 2016)

What is it these calls are requesting when 911 is contacted? Isn't a 911 call a call for someone to defend with the authority that a weapon brings to the scene? Wouldn't it be a disappointment if first responders were unarmed? Even if armed professionals are enroute, potential victims know that outside help may be too slow, and the caller's personal response time can be much shorter, possibly making an important difference.

The driving forces of this decade that have spurred interest in gun ownership to new, unheard-of highs, are often political. We have witnessed turbulence in the United States, unseen since the '60s. During the fall of 2009, our government engaged in Operation Fast and Furious, which conveyed "thousands of semi-automatic firearms" to people in Arizona thought to have links to Mexican drug cartels. (Minter,inForbes,2011www.forbes.com/sites/realsipn/2011/09/28/fast-and-furious-just-might-be-president-obamas-watergate/?)

After thoroughly examining the details of this "reckless operation", author Frank Minter concludes, "Given all the politics and the cover up that even the former ATF director says has occurred, could Operation Fast and Furious have been about anything other than pushing for new gun law?"

More recently, there were riots, protests, looting, property destruction, and threats in our cities from coast to coast leading right up to the November 2020 election! We have been amazed at the erosion of time-honored norms, such as police protection and legal actions against lawbreakers. The occupations of downtown Portland and Seattle went on for weeks, and destroyed businesses, as the mayor and governor looked on with approval. Riots occurred in numerous cities across the nation during the "Summer of Love, 2020".

We have heard politician Beto O'Rourk's rally cry, "H___ yeah, we're going to take your guns!" This threat contributed mightily to additional gun purchases. In gun-owner speak, the reply to that is, "Come get 'em!" On the heels of O'Rourk's statement, came numerous attacks on police and serious calls to defund those local police precincts.

As of this writing, the US has developed a notoriously "porous border". Tens of thousands are streaming across into the US illegally, from all over the globe, as frustrated Border Patrol agents have had their job descriptions rewritten. All this coupled with the Taliban windfall of hundreds of thousands of advanced small-arms weapons, left by the US Military exiting Afghanistan, contribute to a fear of advanced weaponry in the hands of unidentified enemies crossing our southern border.

Understandably, people are considering their self-defense options, and they are pushing gun sales off the charts! Piling on, are the folks who see other benefits to gun ownership. Beyond mere self-defense, firearms are used in shooting sports, hunting, safety in the wild, and competitive shooting. Some guns are collectible; they may be family keepsakes. Some are even considered to be decorative. A few owners consider firearms an investment. For all the reasons above, we Americans love our guns! We have lots of them. The Small Arms Survey of 2018 reported that US civilians own about 393 million firearms, which is roughly 46 percent of all guns owned by civilians globally. Adding to that another estimate of 37 million more in sales for the period from 2019 to mid-year 2021 brings the estimate to 430 million. We have more guns than active cell phones. Almost all estimates state that in the US there are more guns than people! What's up with all this, you may ask. How did gun ownership get so deeply rooted into the American way of life?

1

GUNS IN THE AMERICAN CULTURE

Handguns and Long Guns in American Culture

AMERICA'S LOVE AFFAIR WITH THE HANDGUN began with the Colt in the 1880s and intensified with the arrival of television sets in almost every home in the country in the 1950s. Every Saturday night for almost twenty years, America watched as Matt Dillon (James Arness) swaggered down the main street of the Dodge City set of "Gunsmoke" for the inevitable opening duel with the bad guy. As the camera panned Dillon's sagging hip holster, with his challenger framed in the distant backdrop, to make sure everyone could see that Dillon waited for the bad guy to draw first, the US Marshal dropped him. The marshal accomplished this feat every Saturday night without fail for twenty years. It was a miracle! It's been said that he wore out *seven* 7 ½ inch Colt .45s while saving the West. These show guns have been deemed Hollywood's top collectibles and have sold for more than $50,000 each. (truewest-magazine.com, 'Gunsmoke's Gun for Hire' March18, 2014.)

While television elevated gun slinging to an art form and mesmerized millions, the movie industry piled on as well. Who can forget *American Sniper, True Grit, Diehard, Collateral, Rambo, Sudden Impact,* with Clint Eastwood's famous line, "Go ahead! Make my day!" as he taunted a young punk to give him an excuse to shoot.

Our Millennials have grown up with an annual viewing of *A Christmas Story,* a movie set in a small Indiana town in the 1940s. Everything revolves around nine-year-old Ralphie's business-like campaign for the ultimate gift, an "Official Red Ryder Carbine-Action 200 Shot Range Model Air Rifle". That's a direct quote of what Ralphie tells Santa Clause. There is no back-up plan. His unwavering single-minded determination drives him right through the festivities of Christmas as he struggles through a world that is seemingly stacked against him.

As Ralphie and so many of America's beloved heroes romped across the big and small screens, they effortlessly employed their firearms to subdue the bad guys, save the towns, rescue the damsels, and win the wars, all while inserting firearms early and often into the American psyche as a symbol of power over evil. The overriding lesson, which rings true in real life as well, is that bad guys have guns, so, good guys better have them too, and they must be better at using them.

Would you like to know Hollywood's favorites? Four of the top five guns used in movies are handguns. According to thetruthaboutguns.com post, viewed on 12 May 2021. The most likely handguns you will see in movies are the Luger P08, the M 1911A1, the Glock17, and most frequently seen on screen, is the Beretta 92FS, aka M9.

The Need to Know More

Many of the country's collection of arms are in the hands of well-meaning people who would like to know more about them. Similarly, our seasoned gun owners need to refresh their knowledge and skills at intervals. With so many guns in our environment, it becomes essential that all of us develop a working knowledge for handling them. According to an NPR report on 26 April 2021, 40 percent of sales are to first time gun buyers. The information in *Gun Points,* hopefully, will be a good starting point for new owners, and an informative resource for others. Even if you don't particularly care for guns, reading this will help you hold your own when you find yourself in the company of firearm devotees, and you will, because they are everywhere. Based on your reading this, you might even be able to lay out some esoteric concepts just to rattle their cages. This text is not intended to replace the experience of training under a professional firearms instructor in a secure environment, nor will it replace specific study of the arm(s) you choose to own.

Another goal of this book is to offer an unvarnished look at the significance of this cherished RIGHT to gun ownership, with a respect for the attendant responsibilities. My purpose is to equip the reader with the basics of firearm ownership, a Firearms 101, that is lacking in our schools, universities, and even libraries.

I am breaking a few rules by visiting so many different topics related to gun ownership. A number of these themes could provide material to warrant a separate book. I want to help my readers to a working knowledge of the many ways firearms permeate our existence. Hopefully, the presented material will inspire readers to continue to explore the fascinating world of firearms.

We will review some surprising aspects of firearm discipline. I was astonished to see Assistant District Attorney Thomas Binger in his closing argument, in the Kyle Rittenhouse case of 2021, who, while knowing the proceedings were televised nationally, *pointed the defendant's AR-15 toward the jurors, with a finger on the trigger!* (televised video news report, 15Nov2021 Fox News Primetime) I think he violated all four of the basic safety rules for handling firearms. This guy was the prosecutor in a high-profile firearms case! Apparently, something similar happened with the Alec Baldwin event on the movie set of *Rust* and resulted in one death and another person injured. As of this writing, the latter has not gone to trial, but I'm ready to rest my case! We need to educate the entire nation on basic firearm discipline! With this missive, I want to ricochet around the universe of firearms with you.

Hopefully, you will get a sense of the pervasiveness of firearms in our national habitat. So, hang on! We're going to visit the Supreme Court, the American Wild West, and Olde England in 1605, a firing range and other gun-related venues.

Have you *"dodged a bullet"* lately? Or have you been aware of someone getting *"up in arms"*? These and similar phrases color our language to an astonishing degree. We will examine many of these gun-related phrases in **OUR GUN-LOADED LANGUAGE** installments.

We will mix a little gunpowder, try to get into the collective heads of highway patrolmen, and speculate on the effects of noise on unborn babies when expectant mamas visit the range. We will shoot the bull with some of my friends about what causes "accidental" firearm discharges and discover a contemporary rifle called SCAR. You're going to become intimate with the GCA, NFA, the ATF, the FMJs, the FFLs, Brady, bullpups, Puckle guns, and more! It's a big gun world!

Not that long ago, shooting sports were taught in secondary schools and students brought shotguns to school and placed them in their lockers. Things are very different now and I think we have lost something important to our education and to school safety. The Gun-Free School Zones Act of 1990 made possession of a firearm in a school zone a federal crime, law enforcement excepted. The wisdom of this act is debatable.

News reports sensationalize gun deaths to the point of hysteria, as they massage out important aspects of the stories. In quite a few cases, the public protection systems simply failed their duty; criminals are issued guns against policy, and deaths result.

Even churches in America are arming up, so I will include some thoughts on what to do when things go wrong, as in an active shooter scenario. Also, I have included a brief discussion of first aid for gunshot wounds.

I am constantly teaching and explaining various aspects of gun ownership to customers, acquaintances, and friends, all of whom are the inspiration for this book. I see a wide-ranging lack of gun-handling knowledge in the face of increasing sales. Consequently, we will touch down on as much of this as time and space allow. I am drawing on my years of work in retail firearm sales, my background as a former Navy Corpsman, and my love of the freedoms outlined in the Bill of Rights of the Constitution of the United States of America.

Why Firearms?

Why are firearms the chosen devices used to control desperate situations? Isn't there some other way? For the answer, consider the attributes of handguns and long guns.

They are precise and efficient. Firearms are much less a threat in crowded urban situations where precise control is needed, than say, explosives or poisons. Witness the numerous hostage situations that have been resolved by sniper fire, resulting in one down... and one returned to Mama. What else could deliver this level of lethality to the source of the problem, the hostage taker, and yet, provide safety for the hostage? An incendiary device? Pepper spray? A knife? A social worker? A psychologist? No, none of these is as effective as a precisely placed round.

While firearms are to be respected, certainly, they pose relatively little risk to the handler. Consider the thousands who carry firearms openly and/or concealed every day. It almost never happens that someone is injured by simply carrying a firearm. Firearms are highly durable, portable, concealable, and relatively inexpensive. They do not depend on the weather, electricity, or the internet to boot up. In short, you can depend on them.

It is easy to obsess over the misuse of firearms because there are many tragic examples. However, the order and safety our weapons provide to society, is an unmeasured parameter. One way to get a determination on this is to examine the effect of banning guns, as happens in gun-free zones. It is an easy exercise to track down numerous illegal shooting events that have occurred as armed cowards have fired on innocents gathered in places perceived to be gun-free zones. Likewise, cities with the strictest gun control laws often have the highest gun crime rates.

Another consideration might be an examination of the course of historical events and the plight of societies where guns are forbidden. Australian citizens gave up their firearms during the period from the fall of 1996 to the fall of 1997. The initial elation over the reduction in gun-related mortality has given way to concern for human rights. "Australia is a nation 'that has lost much of its luster in global human rights and values circles over the past 20 years." – political commentator, Greg Barnes, Dec. 2020. (Canaberra's human rights violations deserve wider international attention. globaltimes.cn, pub. 14mar2021) Reportedly, parts of Sydney are currently under martial law. Patrick Henry comes to mind.

It has been said that handheld firearms are obsolete now that we have nuclear weapons. Ironically, our menacing nuclear weapons are stored in facilities protected in part by "heavily armed US troops". (viewed 28sept2021,theconversation.com/why-the-us-has-nuclear-weapons-in-turkey-and-may-try-to-put-the-bombs-away-125477) What could be more important than keeping our nukes secure?

Our Second Amendment Rights protect all the other rights afforded by the Constitution. This God-given right to bear arms comes with a profound responsibility for intelligent handling of the same. I will save for another time my thoughts on slave states and genocide events where civilian ownership of firearms has been forbidden. In a perfect world, we would put away our guns, and enjoy peace, but until that perfect world is achieved, we need our equalizers, our comforters, our firearms.

A Bit of History, and the Right to Bear Arms

The United States of America has more guns in civilian hands than any place on earth. Estimates are that there are more than 400 million firearms in the hands of our free civilians living in the United States. Our tradition of owning firearms dates back to the very beginning of our country as explained by Geza John Vamos in his Jan. 12, 2019, letter to the editor (Posted Jan. 26, 2001) updated, Letter to the Editor of the Sun News: (FB, , 963 shares Twitter?) shared here with permission:

"I am dismayed by what I have been reading, hearing, and seeing on the 2nd Amendment. Some people are calling for curbs on the 2nd Amendment. These people seem to forget that the 2nd Amendment protects the freedom of speech, the press, religion, and assembly. The Founding Fathers realized that an armed citizenry is essential to keep a tyrannical government at bay.

"If you want curbs on the Second Amendment, then prepare yourselves for curbs on freedoms that you are taking for granted now. Expect curbs on your freedom of speech, freedom of the press, freedom of religion, and freedom of assembly. Do not give up rights and freedoms in the hope of trying to eliminate violence. The bad guys do not play by the rules anyway. Why limit the rights of the good guys to protect themselves? What most people fail to realize, because they are not taught it, is the match that ignited America's War for Independence was attempted gun confiscation.

"On April 19, 1775, some 800 British troops were dispatched to Concord, Mass., to arrest Sam Adams and John Hancock and to seize a cache of weapons known to be stored at Concord. When Dr. Joseph Warren sent Paul Revere to warn Pastor Jonas Clark (in whose home Adams and Hancock were staying) the Crown's troops were on their way to arrest the two men and seize the guns at Concord, he (the pastor) alerted his male congregants. About

60-70 men from the Church of Lexington stood armed on the Lexington Green awaiting the Red Coats.

"Upon spotting the citizen militia, a British officer demanded they throw down their arms. They refused; and the British troops immediately opened fire. Eight of the Minutemen were instantly killed. The colonists returned fire in self- defense, and the shot was fired that was heard 'round the world'. By the time the troops arrived at the Concord Bridge, just a few miles away, hundreds of colonists were waiting for them with muskets in hand, and the rest, as they say, is history.

"Make no mistake about it: attempted gun confiscation ignited America's War for Independence. If the federal government attempts to confiscate the guns of the American people. 'There would be a revolution in this country!'

"To quote George Washington, 'If freedom of speech is taken away then dumb and silent we may be taken away like sheep to the slaughter.'

"Wake up from your slumber, people. All our rights and freedoms are in grave danger.'" (Vamos)

2

TOWARD GUN OWNERSHIP

Before You Buy ... Should You?

BEFORE YOU TAKE A FIREARM INTO your home, carefully look things over. Consider the activities of the people who come and go from your habitat. Is it likely that someone, adult or child, or child-like adult, or precocious child who thinks himself an adult, or any impaired person could get access to your firearm without your knowledge? What would likely be the result if an accidental discharge happened at your home? Do you live in an apartment with others living in tight proximity, only separated by standard wall construction? These are things you must consider as you contemplate gun ownership.

Are you willing to bear the expense and hassle involved in safe storage for your firearm under lock and key or lock and code? A locked, fireproof safe is optimal. These are available, but not cheap, at retail sporting stores, websites, and in catalogs. There are many creative, inconspicuous gun safes available. These could help you avoid keeping all your firearms in one safe and help you access your go-to firearm readily in an emergency. If possible, even the gun safe should be hidden behind a false wall, as an extra deterrent to thieves or wannabe users.

In thinking about firearm ownership, you will want to consider all the members of your household. Do you have young children living with you? Even if you have schooled your young ones in firearm safety, it is crucial that you keep any weapons under lock and key or carefully kept code locks, with ammo stored separately.

9

Be mindful of your children's friends or other young relatives who may be visiting.

What of the adults in your household? Is there even a remote chance that an emotionally unstable adult could get access to your firearm and use it to harm self or others? Another hard question you must ask yourself is, are *you* emotionally stable? Are you prone to fits of anger? Have you ever destroyed property or hurt someone in anger? Are you currently in a period of anxiety, depression, or loss? Have you ever tried to hurt yourself, or attempted suicide? Are you restricted from gun ownership as a result of past convictions? Do you party heavily? Use recreational drugs? Use excessive alcohol?

The Decision to Purchase

If you are answering "yes" or "maybe" to these questions, now is not the time to purchase a firearm. You will need to find other ways to secure your homeplace. Shooting sports can wait. You need to take personal responsibility and make decisions based on the reality of your situation. A tragedy happened recently, in a town near me, that resulted in the gunshot death of an unattended four-year-old. While the adults in the home were playing cards and smoking marijuana, the child found a handgun under the sofa cushions. This was preventable. A child is dead. Two adults are in lock-up, facing charges. As you contemplate gun ownership, are you prepared to keep everybody safe? The failure to secure a firearm is a serious matter.

What to Purchase

What will meet your needs? My first advice is to buy a well-made, high-quality firearm. Cheaply made, heavily used, or worn guns are prone to misfiring and safety failure. Heavily used rifles and handguns lose their rifling after years of use; this reduces speed and accuracy. Older shotguns may have mechanism and barrel damage from the many variations of materials loaded. Think of your firearm as an investment. If well-maintained, they hold value and will likely increase in value.

There are literally hundreds of firearm designs. There are numerous crossovers and modifications that make it difficult to describe basic categories of firearms. Depending on the load, a rifle may be used to fire pellets, thereby performing the function of a shotgun. Conversely, some shotguns may on occasion shoot "slugs" which are similar in function to that of rifles. Some shotguns look more like over-sized handguns. These are examples of cross-over designs and functions that blur the lines of broad categories of firearms. There are myriad alterations and modifications in the manufacture of firearms. Mechanisms of action of modern firearms include revolver, break action, bolt action, lever action, pump action, automatic (more for military use), and semi-automatic. There are gas guns, popular for their gentler recoil, and hard-kicking, inertia-driven guns as well.

Also, there are different laws governing different categories of firearms. These categories are established by the Bureau of Alcohol, Tobacco, and Firearms (BATF formerly the ATF). This organization determines what category of firearm each new offering falls into, based on characteristics such as barrel length, presence or absence of a stock, rate of fire, country of origin, and the like.

3

THE LONG GUNS

The Long Guns: Shotguns and Rifles.

LONG GUNS ON AVERAGE ARE HEAVIER, and they require two-handed operation. Generally, the long guns are shotguns and rifles and are not easily concealed. Those classified as shotguns must have a barrel length minimum 18" to 18.5" to be categorized as a long gun. Advantages of these longer barrels is to improve range of fire, velocity, and accuracy. Accuracy improves with long guns; the view through the sites is further out toward the target, which improves the grouping.

OUR GUN-LOADED LANGUAGE

Lock, Stock & Barrel: This is a reference to a complete firearm, a flintlock musket. The "lock" refers to the chamber and firing mechanism. The "stock" is the wooden gunstock. The "barrel" of course is the gun barrel. These three elements complete the package, to imply the whole shebang is in play. The phrase left flintlocks behind long ago and took on a life of its own. Now, it means that everything is included.

For buyers in many states, no permitting through the local Sheriff's Office is required for the purchase of shotguns and rifles. Most states do require a sheriff-issued permit for handguns. Generally, for a long gun purchase, you will need to show proof that you are older than eighteen years, have a valid government-issued ID, and pass a background check. (For the purchase of a handgun, you must be at least twenty-one years of age and some states require a permit to purchase from your local Sheriff's Office, an ID, and a satisfactory background check.) Remember most firearm regulations come from state and local sources. Gun buyers and sellers need to stay informed of these.

A distinguishing feature of long guns, usually, is the presence of a stock. Known as the gunstock, the buttstock, or shoulder stock, the stock functions to stabilize the weapon against the shoulder of the shooter on the dominant eye side. Unfortunately, this also transfers the recoil impact to the shoulder as well. Some shooters invest in specially made shirts with shoulder pads. Most gunstocks come with a rubberized cushion at the base. Historically, gunstocks have been made of hardwood, frequently walnut, and have been used as far back as 1571. When the musket arrived on American soil, the indigenous people were quick to adapt to this new technology. However, when their ammunition was depleted, these warriors found the musket stocks to be effective as war clubs. You can imagine the lethality. (Military.wikia.org, viewed 27 Ap. 2021)

OUR GUN-LOADED LANGUAGE

Flash in the pan: This saying originated in the seventeenth century with the use of flintlock muskets. The firing of a flintlock was accomplished by the action of the cock striking the flint, which delivered a spark to the tiny pan that carried a small amount of gunpowder, which in turn, ignited the charge in the barrel. Occasionally, the powder in the pan ignited, but the charge in the barrel failed to ignite.

This disappointment came to be known as a "flash in the pan." The use of the phrase persists with the meaning that something or someone initially appeared promising but failed to deliver beyond the figurative initial flash. (How to Load and Fire a Flintlock Rifle viewed 21JAn2022BLMORGON also gingersoftware.com/content/phrases/flash-in-the-pan/)

Gunstocks have been decorated with carvings and even gold or silver inlays, making them true investment quality art forms. Conversely, contemporary engineers have taken a pragmatic approach to gunstock construction. The shapes and varieties of gun stocks, of late, are mere frames or rough outlines of the stocks of old. The newfangled gun stocks may be removable. Scandalously, some are even constructed of high-impact plastics, to reduce weight.

Shotguns

Have, you ever heard the "scrrrr-a-atch-cr-aack" sound of a pump shotgun being racked? If you have not, this is worth Googling, or better, stop by a range and listen. This is arguably the most dreaded sounds an intruder will ever hear. The mere sound of racking a shotgun can persuade an invader to rethink plans; helpful, because you save a couple of shells and avoid a clean-up. Upon hearing this scrub of metal on metal, a thoughtful prowler, already in panic mode, will infer: 1) There is a shotgun near and ready. 2) Depending on the load, the operator may be able to spray a wider area than is penetrated by a rifle. It is quite convincing.

Shotguns differ from rifles, in that *generally* they have a larger smooth-bore barrel that *usually* has no rifling. The barrel may vary in length from eighteen and a half inches out to thirty-two inches, depending on the use.

A shotgun having a shorter barrel, less than eighteen and a half inches, is designated by the ATF as a short barrel shotgun or SBS. An SBS is an example of an NFA item and requires a special $200 tax stamp. I caution shotgun owners who may want to shorten a shotgun barrel. This modification can change a legal firearm into an illegal SBS if the required tax stamp has not been secured. According to an Amazon documentary, Randy Weaver of Ruby Ridge fame was initially indicted for "sawing off" one or more shotgun barrels for pay.

Shotguns fire shells and/or slugs, and sometimes other stuff (See the chapter on "Ammunition"). A shotgun shell is basically a small canister loaded with pellets that scatter when fired. Slugs, an alternative form of shotgun ammo, are heavy metallic solid projectiles fired from shotguns. Shotguns are often referred to by the gauge, which is the inside diameter of the barrel, and the same number denotes the size of the shell or slug to be fired. Shotguns are sized as 10-, 12-, or 20-gauge, and rarely 16-gauge. The .410-bore shotgun bears mention as well. Remember, for reasons that are clear to no one, the higher the gauge number, the smaller the bore. The great American favorite is the 12-Gauge. Although "12-gauge" is a unit of measurement, it is enough said; there is no need to add the word "shotgun". Shooters all know what a 12-Gauge is. Almost all firearm manufacturers produce some version of the 12-Gauge, among them: Winchester, Remington, Beretta, Benelli, Mossberg, and others. General types of shotguns include Semi-automatic, Pump, and Break Action. Most shotguns are single barrel; however, there are double-barrel versions that have a "break-open" design that is important in shooting sports.

Firing a shotgun pellet-type shell results in a spray effect on the target. Depending on the situation, it may be desirable to control the pattern of that spray and the concentration of pellets. This is accomplished by use of a choke device aka, choke tube which may be one to four inches in length and screws into the distal tip called the "muzzle" of the shotgun barrel. A choke tube constricts the area of the shot spray and influences the range. The "tighter" the choke the longer the range. Some shotguns are designed with the choke built in. Others may have a variety of screw-in chokes that may be changed by using a wrench. "The Guide to Shotgun Chokes" (1source.basspro.com) likens the choke to a nozzle on a garden hose. Just as the nozzle constricts the flow of water and increases the pressure and distance of the stream of water; similarly, a choke tube compresses and extends the pellet spray of the shotgun. Chokes are classed as Super-Full, Full, Modified, Improved Cylinder, Cylinder, and Skeet.

It has been argued that shotguns are better suited for self-defense in an urban area because the lighter pellet spray particles are less likely to penetrate through wall boards than a bullet from a rifle or handgun. Others vehemently contest this idea. I can only speak from a personal experience where a 12-gauge was accidentally discharged indoors. In that event, the discharge broke through the first interior wall but not through the next wall which was ten feet away. From this experience, I can support either argument!

The history of shotguns winds across continents and through five centuries. By 1790, a British gunsmith, Joseph Manton, the "father of the modern shotgun" was making double barrel shotguns. By the mid-1800s the use of the shotgun was a well-established convention across America.

An American, John Moses Browning (1855-1926) was a prolific designer and the founder of the Browning Arms Company. Mr. Browning is credited with inventing the lever action shotgun, and the pump action style, and numerous other innovations for a variety of weapons. (John Browning-wikip… en.m.wikipedia.org) Many of his older designs such as the 1911 are highly regarded and remain in production today.

There is a nostalgia associated with the older double-barreled break action shotguns. These were carried by the Wells Fargo guards, aka "messengers", who sat by the stagecoach drivers and defended the treasure and economy of our fledgling democracy in the 1800s. Currently, some of those older guns are valued at more than $150,000 each. A new name is being used to dress up these old guns. In some circles they are now referred to as "Coach Guns" to enhance the value, perhaps. Author John Taylor has a book out about all these older shotguns. *Fine Shotguns* has earned a five-star review on Amazon.

OUR GUN-LOADED LANGUAGE

Shotgun wedding: A wedding that takes place due to threats from the bride's family's demand that the groom take responsibility for the bride's pregnancy. Subsequent use of the phrase suggests that a pregnancy preceded the wedding.

While some of the shotguns produced now, in the twenty-first century would look quite familiar to John Browning, he would be astonished by the many new developments. Laser lights, tactical lights, tube magazines, and argon-driven pistons for rapid reloading, and fat price tags are characteristic of many of today's high-tech weapons. The menacing appearance and the designation as "tactical" help with the hype! Some of their descriptors are "Rambo-like", "fastest on the planet", and "Sci-Fi-looking". I will describe a few of the newer ones of interest, from this current sea of available shotgun models. This is not necessarily an endorsement of these items for home defense or sports, though they may be promoted as such.

LTT 1301 Tactical Shotgun by Langdon, a fast-cycling, semi-automatic 12-gauge promoted for home defense. (PIC?) This is a modification of the Beretta 1301. It is very light and kind to the shoulder. Along with a Nordic magazine tube extension to increase ammo capacity out to seven shells, it features rails for mounting lights or a "side saddle" for storing even more shells. Ergonomics are optimized by the MagPul butstock. (langdontactical,com) Expect to pay $1,600 to $1,900. The comparable Benelli M4 sells for approximately $2,000.

Another interesting 12-gauge is the Origin 12 SBS (short barrel shotgun) by Fostech, a semi-automatic 12-gauge shotgun that would look right at home in the hands of the Space Marines in the movie *DOOM*. It has a unique gas system that makes it exceptionally fast cycling, when compared to other semi-automatic shotguns. It is recommended for home defense and close work. The SBS model is a Title 2 weapon that requires an NFA Form 4 tax stamp, which adds $200 to the cost. There is a longer barreled version that does not require the stamp. As of this writing the cost is approximately $3,100 and you get to wait six to eight months for delivery.

For home defense needs, a more affordable, practical, yet dependable 12-gauge shotgun choice would be a Mossberg 500 or Mossberg 590 or a Remington 870. Expect to pay approximately

$400 or more for one of these. You may find that some of these may be in short supply as of this writing.

The Remington Tac 14, and the Mossberg 590 Shockwave are firearms that fall between the category cracks—too big to be a handgun, too short to be a shotgun and lacking a stock; but having 12-gauge pump action all the same. Another, similar 12-guage is the Remington V3 Tac 13 semi-automatic.

These are classified as "Pistol Grip Firearms" by the ATF. The unusual near-horizontal Shockwave Raptor grip, also known as "bird's head pistol grip" doesn't look much like a pistol grip, and it seems a poor substitute for a full stock. *The Havok Journal* states, "Your hand jumps with every shot, and this one is 'not well suited for a beginner.'" The words "nasty recoil" season the report! This is a fun gun—in experienced hands only! (havokjournal.com/national/-security/defense/tac14/)

Roy Chesson, writing for *Gun University* (Jan 11, 2021) reviews another innovative shotgun, the KEL TEC KSG, an intimidating gun by appearance, performance, and reputation. He explains, the KSG simply means Kel Tec Shotgun, and the KS7 are the only shotguns currently produced by Kel Tec. I bring the KSG to your attention because it represents one of several, *bullpup*-style shotguns. These all are designed with the trigger out forward of the action. The benefit is that this gives the firearm a shorter overall length without sacrificing barrel length, thus avoiding legality issues.

Somewhere back in time, someone thought the appearance was like the nose of a bulldog puppy, thus the name, *bullpup*. Go figure! It stuck. Based on Chesson's report, here again, is a firearm better left to experienced hands. He gives it good marks for being compact, and easy to handle with high capacity. On the downside, He reports that the plastic components and the safety feel cheap. He had a design complaint as well, in the way shells are ejected just behind and right of the main grip area, where his right wrist was bombarded! (Chesson, Roy Jan11, 2021Kel Tec Review[2021]:Legit or a Dud gununiversity.com/kel-tec-ksg-review)

Rifles & Carbines

If you are looking for power and accuracy, a longer barreled shooting iron will better meet the need. The long barrel exposes the load to the explosion from the chamber a bit longer, for a greater velocity. Also, with long guns, the view through the sites is a bit further out toward the target, which improves accuracy. Both speed and accuracy are improved by rifling grooves inside the barrel.

A *rifled* gun barrel is one which has spiraling grooves along the inside wall, for the purpose of setting the bullet into a stabilizing spin. The measure of these spirals required to rotate the bullet one full turn is known as "twist rate". A 1:7 twist means one full rotation of the bullet every seven inches traveled inside the barrel. You will find rifling down the barrels of rifles, handguns, and even some shotguns. The rifling sets up a spinning motion that continues in flight. This keeps the tapered nose of the bullet forward. It's the same principle that is demonstrated when a quarterback puts a spin on a football for a long pass. Bullets fired from a smooth or worn barrel tend to tumble in flight and go off course. The internal diameter of a rifle barrel is generally narrower than a shotgun barrel. The combination of rifling and the narrow barrel vastly improve range, dynamics, and accuracy.

A carbine is a rifle having a shorter barrel, usually less than twenty inches. According to our friends at the ATF, a carbine or other rifle having a barrel shorter than sixteen inches is classified as an SBR (short barrel rifle). SBRs are NFA items and require a special tax stamp. The carbine may have other features that make it lighter, and it may use a lighter form of ammunition. It has been helpful for troops who travel on foot or work in tight spaces. A carbine style rifle in a common pistol caliber like 9mm is a workable choice for home defense. It will have the advantage of reduced recoil and easy maneuverability. These can be set up to your liking with special sites such as a red dot or a holographic site, or even iron sites. These are fun and affordable to shoot at the practice range as well.

OUR GUN-LOADED LANGUAGE

Top gun: The one who is most talented, most capable, most respected, and perhaps most dreaded. This is also a movie title.

AR-15

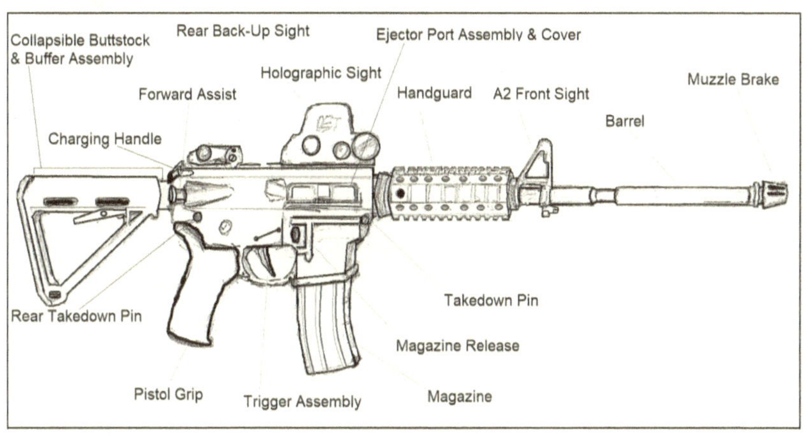

The most popular rifle prototype in the US is the AR-15, a semi-automatic firearm. Do not be confused about the "AR". It stands for *ArmaLite Rifle,* not the wildly fear-producing label of *ASSAULT RIFLE!* The name "AR-15" is a trademark owned by Colt, however the original, slightly larger design, was produced in the '50s by a Marine named Eugene Stoner. Stoner's design is now in the public domain, meaning it can be widely copied by many manufacturers. These producers use a different name and add hyphen 15, such as the M&P-15, manufactured by Smith & Wesson. Semi-automatic simply means the trigger must be squeezed once for each round that fires, whereas, with a fully automatic weapon, the mechanism continues to fire with one continuous compression of the trigger. The fully automatic capability is useful in warfare. Estimates vary, but there may be as many as 10 million AR-15 (ArmaLite Rifle) style firearms in the hands of civilians in the US. A noted authority and gun reviewer, a YouTube celebrity, a gentleman who calls himself Hickok45, Greg Kinman appeared on the Fox Network, Tucker Carlson Tonight, on April 23, 2021, to help clear up some of the misunderstandings regarding the AR-15s. Here are some take-away points from that interview:

- AR-15s are popular because they are "so reliable".
- AR-15s are preferred because they have relatively less recoil and they have an adjustable stock.
- AR-15s are excellent firearms for sport, hunting, competition, and home defense.
- He noted that in areas where AR-15s are common, usually the rural areas, crime rates trend lower.
- Since AR 15s available to civilians are *not* fully automatic, they do not qualify as "assault weapons", nor are they weapons of war according to Hickok45. However, our military has a similar weapon, the M16, select fire, and the M4, select fire.

While most shooting crimes, particularly those in the inner cities are carried out using handguns, AR-15 style weapons have, on rare occasions, been used by criminals or mentally ill shooters in multiple mass shootings. In the event of a mass shooter scenario, with an AR-15, the load capacity can be readily altered immediately. There is a magazine release button on the right side of most AR-15s just above the trigger guard. A quick tap of this spring-loaded control immediately causes the magazine to drop out, leaving the shooter with only one remaining chambered round. The hero who might attempt this maneuver in an active shooter scenario, should simultaneously force the gun barrel toward a safe direction while ejecting the magazine. Somebody please kick the ejected magazine out of reach! Any others willing to pile on at this point should do it. Interrupting the shooter may enable potential victims to escape.

OUR LOADED GUN LANGUAGE

How Often Have You Heard "Son of a Gun"?

It might be translated, "I'm surprised!" At other times, it is used as a disparaging label, a half click from insulting one's mother. Usually, it is a phrase used to tease a friend. This saying gets plenty of exercise these days, but it may have originated during feudal times in England. It was thought to have been used by knights of the period who resented those using early firearms rather than proper weapons like swords and spears. Another source attributes the phrase to children who were born on British warships. During the 1800s, wives were allowed to accompany British sailors at sea. The wives delivered and suckled their babies under the ship's gun carriage, where they would be out of the way. A son born at sea was a "Son of a Gun". The birth was recorded in the ship's log as such.

Snipers – The Long Gun Experts

The work of a sniper is intriguing. Often the assignment is to take out an opposing sniper who is equally equipped and has a similar mission. What could be more gut wrenching? The legendary snipers of our armed services have been and are now the most intensive users of long guns, their sniper rifles. In addition to their natural talent for long shots, snipers must be able to go it alone for hours, sometimes days, without backup. They may be called upon to infiltrate enemy territory alone, carrying rifles and ammo. They must be able to lie in wait for hours, gazing through a scope, a perfect still life in camo. No scratching, sneezing, wiping away sweat, or batting insects!

Alternatively, they may serve in heavily populated close circumstances where even children may be held as human shields. They are required to make decisions in less time than the next heartbeat. Despite the terrifying circumstances of their service, many of them have displayed colorful personalities and continued meaningful lives after their sniper days.

Their assignments might entail taking out a given target, or overseeing troop movements and providing safe cover. The dreaded snipers are seldom understood or appreciated, but when needed, they are an enormous asset to our battle efforts.

"The very word, 'sniper,' seems to stir passionate reactions on the left. The criticism misses the fundamental value that snipers add to the battlefield. Snipers engage individual threats. Rarely, if ever, do their actions cause collateral damage. Snipers may be the most humane of weapons in the military arsenal. The job also takes a huge emotional toll on the man behind the scope. The intimate connection between the shooter and the target can be hard to overcome for even the most emotionally mature warrior. The value of a sniper in warfare is beyond calculation." (Rorke Denver, *The United States of "American Sniper"* 27JAN2015. U.S. News, *Wall Street Journal*)

Though the identities and activities of currently active-duty snipers are classified, there are great stories, now unclassified, of many of them from our military history. Though they come from various backgrounds, most began their shooting careers during childhood, hunting, often alone, to provide food for their families or shooting predators to protect livestock.

USMC Sgt. Carlos Norman Haithcock II crossed enemy lines in Viet Nam crawling for four days to get within 700 yards to dispatch a high-value target. He made it back to safety. Navy Seal Brandon Webb, a certified SEAL sniper, after many deployments, became the course manager for the Navy program that trained Chris Kyle. Chief Petty Officer Webb went on to author several books.

Sgt. 1st Class Joshua Olson managed to return to service despite losing a leg. Despite the injury, he was later assigned to an Army Marksmanship Unit as a marksman and instructor. (Lewis C. Lin, PeopleMaven, *The Seven best snipers in Military History, military.com/history/top-7-marksmen-us-military.html/amp/* online 07MAR2022)

White Feather, aka, Gunnery Sgt. Carlos Hathcock, known for the white feather he wore in the band of his helmet, served during the Vietnam War. His most famous shot eliminated an enemy sniper named "Cobra". Reportedly, he precisely placed a shot down through the scope of the Cobra's rifle. This shot could only have happened as the Cobra took aim back at Hathcock. A commercial version of the M25, that uses a 7.62 NATO or a .308 Winchester cartridge and shoots out to 900 meters, was named the *White Feather* in his honor.

Another Vietnam War veteran, Chuck Mawhinney is said to have single-handedly out-gunned sixteen enemy soldiers who were converging on him. He used an M40A1 rifle, a bolt-action not unlike the one he used as a kid in Oregon!

Navy SEAL Chris Kyle, aka "the Legend", saved the lives of countless American soldiers in Iraq. Clint Eastwood produced a block-buster movie, *American Sniper,* about the life of the Legend. Kyle was shot to death in Texas in 2013 by a Marine he was trying to help. "His funeral procession stretched more than 200 miles across Interstate 35 in Texas. (*Most Famous American Snipers in History*, Range 13MAY2015 therange702,com/blog/most-famous-american-snipers-in-history/)

These are only a few of the great American Snipers who have served in the toughest and most dangerous assignments imaginable. We owe them all a debt of gratitude. Another sniper of note is Lyudmila Pavlichenko of Ukraine who fought Nazis during WWII. Her story is covered in the chapter, "A Word to Women."

The statistics on snipers only tell us the "confirmed" and "probable" kills. We will never have the count of how many lives were saved by their efforts. The role of the sniper continues into the twenty-first century. As President Zelenskyy of Ukraine listed requests for the war effort against the Russian invasion of Ukraine, he asked for MIGS, Javelins, Stingers, and *sniper rifles*, exemplified by the Remington M40.

4

HANDGUNS AND PISTOLS

The Handgun Revolution

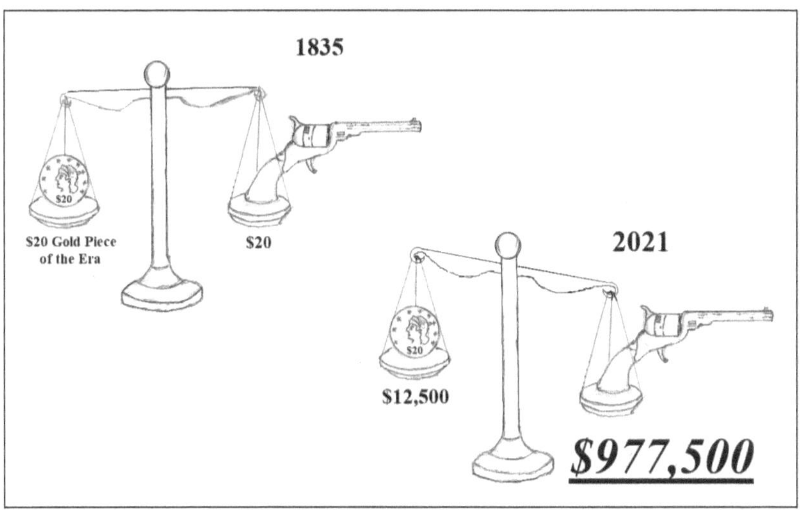

HANDGUNS BECAME POPULAR IN THE US when Samuel Colt secured a patent and became the first to mass-produce a revolutionary repeating firearm, the Colt Paterson Revolver, in 1835. (Gun Timeline/History PBS.org, viewed 13 NOV2021) By 1873, the revolver, along with a holster and a supply of ammunition could be purchased for a $20 gold piece. Currently, any one of those 2,800 Colt Patersons originally produced, is valued at $977,500. (ftknox. com, viewed on 12 May, 2021.) The recent list price of an 1873 issue $20 gold piece in flawless condition is only $12,500 (https://.

cmi-gold-silver.con on 12 May 2021). *The gold piece is worth* only *01.25% of the value of the gun!*

A collector once gave the following reply when asked about his extensive gun collection:

"Guns are the currency of the future." – Paul DeSessa, 1992

Revolvers

Revolvers are a long-standing American favorite, easily identified by the rotating cylinder positioned between the grip and the barrel and directly above the trigger guard. Most revolvers are well-built and dependable when properly maintained. They may be a bit pricey but worth the investment.

Colt's genius cylinder design initially held a five-round load. Currently, a revolver can be loaded with five or six rounds. Some rare varieties hold eight or more rounds. Revolvers seem to be a bit easier for a beginner to understand and operate. A *single-shot revolver* must be cocked back and have the trigger pulled for each shot. A *semi-automatic revolver* fires with each trigger pull. The cocking is automatic. With *double action*, the shooter may manually cock the gun, which makes for an easier trigger pull, or he or she may simply pull the trigger as with the semi-automatic. A semi-automatic revolver can be fired repeatedly with one hand, leaving a free hand to open doors and/or lift a baby.

An amazing revolver described as *fully automatic*, is one that continues firing as long as pressure is on the trigger. These are rare and out of production. An example is the Union Automatic Revolver, manufactured in Ohio and discontinued in 1912.

Criticism of revolvers include 1) The cylinders don't hold as many rounds as a spring-loaded magazine. 2) Reloading is slow compared to a magazine style firearm. The slow reloading is improved by using a *speed loader* or a *moon clip*. 3) The trigger pull may be stiff unless it has a single action vs double action option. The single action mode gives an easier trigger pull, though it requires manually cocking the exposed hammer. A stiff trigger pull reduces accuracy.

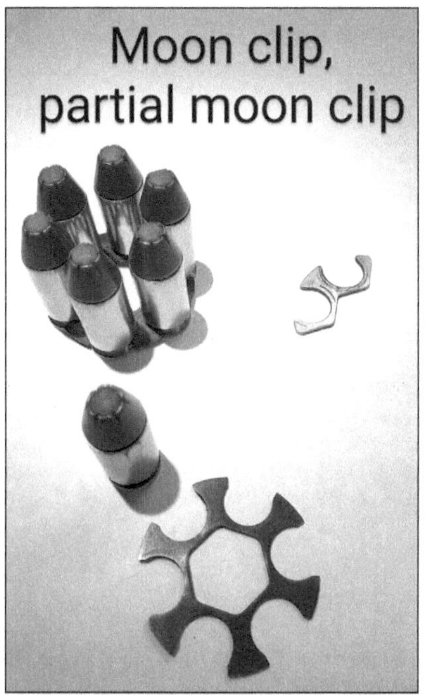

A moon clip is a thin reusable metal form that holds groups of cartridges together so they can be loaded simultaneously. If a moon clip is used, the firearm chamber will need a slight recessed space to accommodate it. Some revolvers are sold with moon clips included—the Smith & Wesson Governor is an example. After all rounds are spent, the moon clip allows for removal of all the cartridge casings together, shortening the reload time, and making it easy to collect spent cartridges for reloading. (Remember the ammo shortage.) Another advantage of the moon clip is related to the fact that most revolvers require ammo with a rim around the base; otherwise the cartridge slides too far forward in the chamber space. When a rimless cartridge is gripped and loaded using a moon clip, the problem is averted. For example, the Governor, mentioned above, accepts three different loads. One of them, the rimless .45 ACP, only holds its position when secured by a moon clip. Hickok45 recommends spinning the entire cylinder in place just after loading, if a moon clip is used. If it spins smoothly, it shows the moon clip is not warped. Moon clips can accommodate all the rounds to be loaded, (five or six max depending on the revolver) Partial moon clips can fit two or three cartridges You can order extra moon clips and load them with cartridges or shells in advance of an outing. Remember you only need these clips and speed loaders with revolvers.

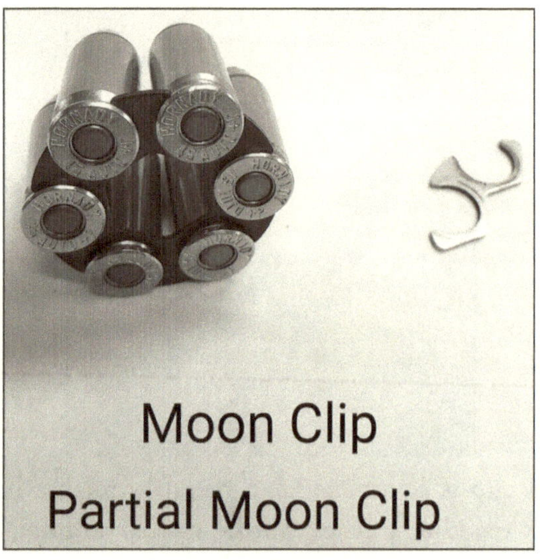

Magazine fed handguns can be loaded quicker and with more rounds, but getting the spring-loaded magazines ready can be a pain. Because you are working against the very strong spring, the more rounds you load, the harder it becomes to overcome the resistance, AND it is possible to get the cartridges in backward! With the revolver, it is easy to see which way the cartridge goes!

A device known as a "speedloader" has been used as well to improve revolver reload intervals. Like the moon clip, the speedloader sets the six cartridges up to be loaded into the revolving cylinder all in one motion. Unlike the moon clip, the speedloader releases the cartridges after loading and the device is removed before firing commences. The speed loader is no help for the rimless cartridge.

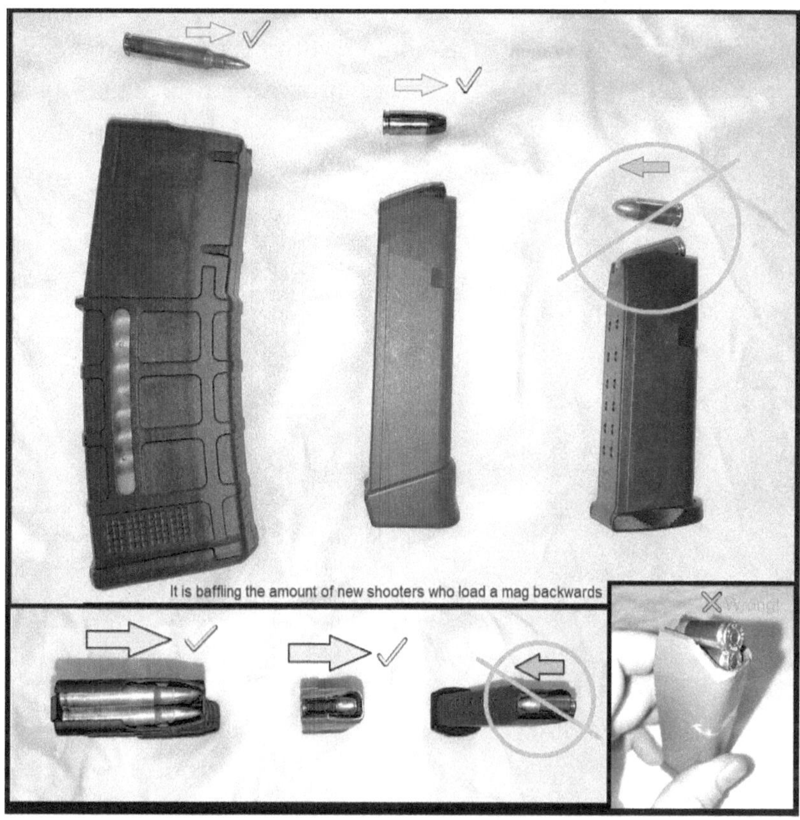

The revolver design is a favorite due to its dependability and the fixed barrel design. Unlike magazine loaded handguns, a revolver will not go "out of battery". Stay with me here, this is not about any kind of battery that supplies power. The phrase means that if or when the slide on a magazine-loaded semi-automatic is out of position, the gun cannot be fired.

Suppose you are in a struggle with an attacker and your handgun is pushed into the bad guy's torso. Any pressure on the slide may render the gun inoperable. This will not happen with the trusty fixed-barrel revolver because there is no slide mechanism. If on the other hand, during a tussle, the barrel is pointed your way, a bit of displacement of the slide, which functions as a safety, might be a good thing.

Revolvers are a favorite back-up gun. They are often carried by off-duty law enforcers. A snub-nosed revolver is compact and great for concealed carry. Some favorite revolver makers include Ruger, Kimber, K6s, Smith and Wesson, FN 503, and Colt.

No discussion of revolvers would be complete without a review of the much-in-demand Smith & Wesson Governor, mentioned above. The amazing thing about this revolver is that the six chambers of the cylinder can take any of three different loads all at the same time! The mix can include the big .45 Colt cartridges, the shorter .45 ACP rimless cartridges if they're on a moon clip, and which normally are used for semi-automatic firearms, and .410 shells which contain various loads. This could be a big advantage if there is a shortage of your preferred ammo. For self-defense at fairly close range, the .410 shells, loaded with four pellets or a slug with shot pellets is recommended for use with the "Gov'nah", as it is affectionately called.

Though the Governor looks fat and menacing, it checks in at only 29.6 ounces due to the scandium alloy frame. The fact that you can load cartridges and shells together is great for dealing with close-up pests while remaining ready for bigger stuff. The Smith & Wesson Governor is an exceptional candidate for camping, or for use as a hunting sidearm, or for car carry. "The Gov'nah" is a strong contender for open carry, and some say concealed carry as well (More on concealed carry in Chapter 6). Dig down deep; it's a bit pricey at $750 to $900 as of this writing.

According to James M. Volo writing for Quora, revolvers like the Smith & Wesson Model 19 were popular choices for decades for law enforcers and private owners alike. LEOs (law enforcement officers) started to rethink the revolver after the 1970 Newhall Incident where four California Highway Patrol Officers were killed in less than five minutes by two suspects. Review and analysis of the Newhall case found that attempts to reload revolvers while under fire contributed to the loss of the lives of these patrolmen.

Another case that helped to turn the tide against revolvers for law enforcement was the infamous Miami Shootout of 1986. The eight FBI agents, armed mostly with revolvers, were nearly overwhelmed by two bank robber/murderers armed with one 12-gauge shotgun, two .357 Magnum handguns, and one .223 Mini-14 rifle. Two agents lost their lives and five were injured. The bad guys both died of police inflicted gunshot wounds. The magazine-loaded Mini-14 rifle in the hands of one of the bad guys led to *all* the deaths and injuries among the eight agents. The shooter was able to fire the Mini-14 "…so fast that one agent later reported it was shooting full automatic. It wasn't." (James M. Volo, In the US why did police switch from revolvers to semi-automatic pistols? Quora. com/Are-there-any-examples-of-semi-automatic-revolvers-other -than the-Webley-Fosbery, viewed online 12FEB2022)

The tragic irony here is that the guy firing the smallest caliber ammo out gunned all those heavier loads. Events like these have led law enforcers and military people to gravitate toward maga-zine-loaded semi-automatic and automatic handguns rather than revolvers.

Some of the most popular handguns include the Springfield XD, the Ruger Gp 100, the KelTec PMR-30, the Glock 19, the Sig Sauer P365, the Taurus Judge, the Ruger LCP, the ATI GSG 1911, the Sig Sauer P320, the Smith & Wesson 442, and the list goes on. (The Gun Source, The Top 15 Most Popular Handguns in the USA, thegunsource.com as viewed 21Sept2021) Handguns are desirable for their price and portability. Also, these smaller fire-arms can be stored in smaller spaces, allowing greater economy in the purchase of a gun safe.

As you consider the purchase of a handgun, it might be helpful to know what firearms are being carried by some of the elite orga-nizations. As of June 21, 2018, the Texas Rangers carry a SIG SAUER P320, an M4 carbine, or a shotgun. (nypd.fandom.com/ wiki/NYPD Weapons, as viewed on 14 May 2021). US Special Forces may carry any of an assortment of carbines, submachine guns, pistols, sniper rifles, rocket and missile launchers, and, yes, even shotguns. (US Special Operations, americanspecialops.com, as viewed 13 July 2021) In addition to all this, you can only imagine what advanced tech secret stuff those guys carry. (sofrep.comgre-attexas-rangers, by Amy Guide, viewed 14 May 2021) The NYPD packs a Glock 19 as well as an M4 carbine or a shotgun. (nypd. fandom.com/wiki/NYPD Weapons, viewed on 14 May 2021)

ATF Special Agents and the ATF Special Response Teams, folks who should know a bit about firearms, will be issued Glock M19s, Colt M4 assault rifles and other firearms. (en.m.wikipedia.org/wiki/Bureau_of_Alcohol,_Tobacco_Firearms_and_Explosives, viewed 28Sept2021)

Where the handguns fall short, is in long range accuracy, due to the shorter barrel. If you are new to shooting a handgun, it is important, as you are shooting, to focus on the bead at the end of the barrel and less on the down-range target. Your eye should focus clearly on putting the bead evenly in the site and the down-range target will be less focused. Just like when you shoot photos, you should be relaxed and still, exhale halfway while still focused on the site as you give the trigger a steady gentle squeeze, so gentle that you are surprised by the discharge. This will improve your accuracy. Ask a certified instructor to coach you.

Per GunPolicy.org, May 14, 2021, the number of privately owned handguns in the US is somewhere between 111,000,000 and 114,000,000. The number of handguns purchased in the US is far greater than the number of firearms classified as shotguns or as rifles. Handguns and pistols are popular due to the convenience of easy portability and storage. As the name suggests, handguns are designed to be operable using only one hand, leaving the other hand free to protect a child, open a door, or for other activity while maintaining aim on the subject. That said, when possible, a two-hand grip provides better stability and accuracy when using a handgun. You should expect your instructor to teach the two-hand grip when you attend handgun classes. I strongly recommend shooting classes for everyone eligible to own a firearm.

The maximum range of accuracy for handguns is about 100 to 110 yards (100 meters), which is approximately the length of a city block. The action of handguns is usually *semi-automatic*; that is, the gun fires one round for each time the trigger is pulled, with no need to manually eject the round or to reload. After each cartridge is fired, the next one is automatically transferred into the firing chamber. The ammo is fed into the chamber of a handgun by a spring-loaded magazine or in the case of a revolver, rotating preloaded cylinder. Revolvers typically hold a maximum of five or six cartridges. Spring-loaded magazines used in handguns typically hold a dozen or so rounds. Practically all firearm manufacturers produce handguns as a popular part of their collections. Some names that come to mind are Springfield, Ruger, SIG, Colt, Smith & Wesson, Henry, Beretta, Glock, Walther, and FN.

5

THOUGHTS ON CONCEALED CARRY

Why Concealed Carry?

THE POPULARITY OF CONCEALED CARRY (CC), aka "carry", is confirmed by multiple sources estimating that more than 21 million of us are credentialed to carry concealed firearms. This figure does not include those who live in the twenty-one *constitutional carry* states where no formal permitting is required.

One reason to conceal your firearm is that guns are of high value to bad guys and are best kept on your person and out of sight. CC is seen as an equalizer in environments where thugs may pounce. Another argument is conceptual, that is, the potential for armed individuals to be in a crowd mix is thought to be a deterrent to violent criminals. And lastly, keeping your gun with you is the best way to be sure that no unauthorized person has access to it. CC is becoming more popular as the crimes escalate.

Another reason for CC over Open Carry (OC) is that it gives the bearer confidence without the hype that goes with a firearm on public display. In my experience, CC is preferable to OC because the latter excites curiosity in some people and fear in others. Once, when I was in a checkout line, a teenaged cashier noticed my pistol and was far more interested in the caliber of my firearm than he was in checking my groceries.

On a different occasion, when I carried openly (OC), I had finished my shopping; and, just as I made my way out the grocery store exit, a deputy came rushing in. It seemed odd. I had been all around inside the store and there was no disturbance. I wondered

37

if some gun-fearing individual had noticed my open carrying and called for law enforcement. This was uneventful; there was no need to explain myself. The point is that the mere sight of a gun is troubling to some people. CC eliminates a lot of nonsense.

The decision to apply for a Concealed Carry permit should be made after great deliberation. I agree with many points offered by David Maccar in his paper called *There is Far More to Concealed Carry Than Just Buying a Handgun. (You need the proper training and mindset before you decide to concealed-carry a handgun. Here's what you need to know. Craft Holsters publication 10 JUN 2021.)* With the exception of a point on page 4 about the wisdom of taking advice from the salesperson, I recommend this six-page read for anyone interested in concealed carry. Maccar leads off with, "It's a serious commitment that will impact pretty much everything someone does outside their home, from the clothes a person wears and how they wear them to the way they get into a car and buckle a seatbelt, to the exact mechanics of picking something up off the floor—or it should." The author walks you through demographics and what motivates people to consider CC. As he explains many practical aspects of CC, he quotes heavily from trainer and U.S. Army Delta Force officer, Kyle Lamb, and from trainer Dave Hartman of Gunsite Academy in Arizona. The article covers everything from "mindset" to practical aspects.

There is even instruction on how to handle a trip to the loo without taking off the holster and firearm. Don't laugh. This is undeniably a high-risk event where the carrier may be tempted to lay the gun aside briefly. Minor distractions happen. They always do. A text message, a knock on the door, or even a random thought could cause you to walk away from your pistol, only to return later and find it missing. It's best to keep it on you at all times when you are out.

Pardon My Rant!

I take issue with Maccar's statement, p.4, "Don't just listen to the kid behind the gun counter…" Wow! Where do I begin? Before you reject the expertise of the salesperson, consider the following:

- Front line sales personnel rack up thousands of hours of carry experience, concealed and open.
- Sales personnel interact constantly with firearms owners of all genres.
- Safety is the overarching concern in a place filled with firearms and ammo, and which is *open to the public, no appointment necessary.* The salesperson must be aware of safety, the rules of safety, and alert to breaches of safety, without fail. Those of us in gun sales are expected to safely carry, with careful attention to our own techniques and gun etiquette. Mr. Maccar has well said, "Carrying a gun is a lot of work." In addition to minding our own guns, there is the added concern for the gun habits of the armed strangers streaming through our doors. I have had the experience of a nurse, no less, bringing her firearm into our store and absentmindedly pointing it at me. Your salesperson will have a heightened awareness and can provide valuable feedback.
- The salesperson will have knowledge of a huge number of firearms, the best uses for them, and the appropriate ammo and accessories.
- The sharing and teaching go on endlessly.
- A good fit is a win-win for both buyer and seller. It is important in sales that we assess a buyer's knowledge and make appropriate recommendations, which may include advice that you delay the purchase. Also, there are physical characteristics of the buyer that influence which gun(s) may be right. The seller may be able to guide you to something you had not thought about.
- The "kid behind the counter" of necessity has a working knowledge of constantly changing gun laws and will

have clearance to access the NICS system for background checks. This includes knowledge of what credentials are required for the purchase of a gun. The salesperson must know the law and guide the purchases, yet assiduously avoid any appearance of giving legal advice. The correct forms must be prepared and purchases recorded. Special orders and online purchases must be relayed by way of the FFL and carried out according to legal standards.

- "The kid" needs to have the ability to gently, but firmly say "no" to a customer whose demeanor is incompatible with safe and legal gun handling. This may include people who appear to be chemically imbalanced, people whose credentials are questionable, and people who give any hint that the firearm might be misused. Our careful assessment of a potential buyer's demeanor can benefit everyone, including the buyer. Your sales rep has to be alert, confident, capable and knowledgeable.

- In addition to the salesperson's skill in serving people of varying levels of gun discipline, there are other gun-related issues for which their knowledge base can benefit the buyer.

- The gun-seller vocation is unlike any other form of retail sales. Along with attending to the responsibilities above, the salesperson will welcome the public with a relaxed, reassuring, and encouraging greeting, trying in every reasonable way to accommodate needs. A salesperson knows that any rise in tension in that environment needs to be quickly and gently resolved.

- We support the sale of firearms because we believe in your right to exercise the God-given freedoms guaranteed by the Constitution. We happily enable firearms to be placed in the hands of law-abiding citizens because it is the right thing to do. We see and know a lot about matching firearms to buyers. We are NOT about "matching XYZ guns they can't sell." Anyway, there aren't any of those. If anything, the problem is in keeping adequate stock available. I share these thoughts in hopes of helping you to understand the resource you have in the people, "behind the counter". You might want to listen to what they have to say.

"You can't just ask customers what they want and then try to give it to them. By the time you get it built, they'll want something new."
—Steve Jobs

Concealed Carry is only practical for handguns and pistols. Here are two bestsellers for CC. The Sig P365, has a patented double-stack capacity and is easily concealed. It is listed at approximately $500. The Glock 19 is larger, but also easily concealable. The Glock is retail priced at approximately $550. There are other fine concealable handguns, too numerous to mention. According to Robert Kaiser, writing for ppss-group.com, Facebook, and Twitter, Federal Air Marshalls carry a Sig Sauer P250 Compact. These guys need their weapons to be perfectly concealed, yet reliable, for obvious reasons.

The CC Process

If or when you become interested in a CC permit, your process will vary by state. Consult your local law enforcement permit office for the process for your area. Some states provide blanket permission for concealed carry to any legal gun owner, without issuing a specific license to carry. This is known as *constitutional carry*.

States that require specific CC licensure will likely require you to successfully complete a specified number of hours of approved CC instruction, preferably with supervised hands-on experiences. Watch out for scammers using deceptive text messages. They may offer bogus instruction and certification, or they may say, "Your concealed carry papers are ready," and ask you to click the link. Don't click it, and don't provide any personal information. According to Sheriff Joey Lemons of Stokes County, NC, "Sheriffs' offices will never send text messages to request any information from residents." (Sheriff Joey Lemons *Concealed Handgun Permit*

Scam, North Carolina Sheriffs' Association newsletter vol. 18, Issue 2 Summer 2021 www.ncsheriffs.org.) Report scams immediately.

With your legitimate Certificate of Completion in hand, you will complete a CC certificate. Your next step will be to contact your local sheriff's office to be fingerprinted and get a background check. You may be asked to authorize a review of your health records. Then you wait. This could take up to ninety days or longer. In my state, CC verification cards are held at the sheriff's office for pickup. Depending on the state, your permit may include a photo. The waiting period is a good time to review state and local gun laws. These laws may include restrictions on knives as well as other lethal weapons all written in with the gun laws. In my state, CC is prohibited when consuming alcohol regardless of location—something to think about.

You should be aware that the CC data is often linked to your vehicle license tag number. When you are pulled over for a traffic infraction, it is likely that the officer will have prior knowledge of your CC permit before approaching your vehicle. Concealed carry, open carry, or the presence of any firearm anywhere in your vehicle will govern your actions at a traffic stop. This brings us to the topic of gun owner behavior at a traffic stop. This will be covered in test answer #7 of the **What are the Regs?** Test, p. 103.

From the time your Concealed Carry permit is approved, life changes. You will need to have unbroken self-control. You will learn to walk away from escalating situations, as soon as possible, especially from those that don't involve you. You will need to drive more carefully and more defensively and control any tendency toward road rage. You will need to be alert to the environments where CC or OC is prohibited such as schools, hospitals, bars, federal buildings, including the post office, and the grounds around them, and adjust your habits to comply. You will change in these ways because the power you are packing can be devastating, life-changing, or life-ending.

Provocative situations are circumstantial, conditional, unpredictable, and never ideal. As someone who carries, you will act with the understanding that shooting another human being or even somebody's pet should happen only as an absolute last resort. Read about the 1992 Ruby Ridge Idaho standoff that, according to one account, began with the killing of a family pet.

No matter how thoroughly justified the use of your firearm, a shooting will be a mess in many ways. If the person fired upon was unarmed, the defense becomes infinitely more difficult. The person with the weapon will likely be judged as having had an advantage. This is not to say that you should never fire your weapon in defense of self or others whose lives are at risk. The purpose of CC is to protect the good guys. If you want a couple of good reads on what happens, the case of George Zimmerman and the case of Kyle Rittenhouse may interest you.

In the circumstance of having to use your firearm, the legal process will be an expensive major hassle. As a fourth step in obtaining your CC permit, I recommend that you invest in a legal retainer specifically for gun owners. US Law Shield and CCW Safe or others may meet your needs. The peace of mind will be worth the expense.

Pepper spray, in addition to your firearm, may be an option to consider as you think about self-defense. You should stay away from any spray container that looks or feels like a gun. In the heat of the moment, any confusion can result in unintended injury. Read the defense statements made by former officer Kim Potter, of Minnesota during her trial in December 2021.

Let Me Count the Ways...

People are often surprised by the many ways CC can be accomplished. Investigate these early; narrow down the method of carry that would be best for your circumstances and body type before purchasing an expensive gun/holster/belt setup. Most sellers don't allow the return of leather or cloth holsters, which are not the best anyway.

Waistband Carry

Waistband carry requires a belt or belly band with a holster. This is the most common method of concealed carry. The holster may be attached either inside the gun belt or band (IWC, inside waistband carry) or outside the waistband (OWC) at a number of points around the circle of the belt. To understand the positioning on the gun belt or band, imagine looking down on a circular waistband with 12 o'clock at the point nearest the belly button. Drawing the handgun will require both hands, one hand to sweep away the overhanging shirt or jacket, and the other hand to remove the gun from the holster. In outside carry, IWC, during the process of drawing the firearm, you may notice more movement of the muzzle as the gun is removed from the holster. This happens because the holster is only secured by the clips or belt slots, leaving the lower portion loose.

4 to 5 o'clock inside waistband carry, IWB, my current preferred method. This position for carry is comfortable for more body types when the optimal holster is in place. It keeps the firearm conveniently away from forward activities like driving or working at a desk. Another advantage is that it allows for an easy ergonomic draw. The gun is positioned relatively close to the dominant hand. Disadvantages include: a) It is hard to draw from the seated position. b) During the draw, the gun bore will flag the user's lower extremity for a milli-second. c) This is not *the* fastest method of drawing but it is among the top three. d) The firearm is not in the field of vision of the person carrying, nor is he or she able to see anyone approaching from behind who may be noticing a bulge from the back side of their waistline.

Appendix carry

Placing the holster at 1 to 2 o'clock, for right-handers or at the 10 to 11 o'clock position for lefties, is known as appendix carry. Appendix carry is a "natural" easy position for carrying concealed that gives quick access. It simply means that the pistol and holster are positioned forward of the hip, in line with the appendix, or on the contralateral side, forward of the left hip. It can be inside the waistband or out. It is not comfortable in a sitting position. It may not work well for some body types. Some disadvantages include: a) Any movement in or out of the holster involves some risk. Clothing or a finger can inadvertently enter the trigger guard. You don't want that. b) When returning the gun to the holster, the muzzle will point toward the femoral artery and your wedding tackle. Re-holster carefully, keeping the shirt tail out of the trigger guard. This is important.

Small of the Back Carry.

With the holster positioned at the small of the back, "SOB carry", is often used for a backup gun. It is uncomfortable, and it causes a slower draw. The biggest concern may be the proximity of the gun, a substantial piece of hardware, so close to the lumbar spines. (Sam Hooker, *Small of the Back Carry Easy Concealment or Injury Waiting to Happen?* USACarry in Articles ConcealedCarry viewed 29JAN2022) The author's concern is that the carrier may be knocked over backward or fall backward onto the low-slung gun attached in the area of the lumbar spine and outflow nerves. He asserts that he is aware of this happening with some frequency, especially to law enforcers. We're talking about a crush injury to nerves that help with bowel function, bladder function, and sexual performance… I'm out.

Belly Band Carry.

With this method a wide elastic band encircles the upper abdomen. A small, light firearm will be needed for comfort and consistent positioning. Belly band carry may be the best option for car carry, or for times when a belt is not worn. Wheelchair dependent people may want to consider this method of carry. Be conscious of the mechanics of the draw from belly band carry. Trigger discipline is critical.

Ankle Carry.

It will be tricky to get this right, especially in a sitting position where trousers tend to rise off the ankle, revealing the pistol. Ankle carry only works with a small piece. The draw will be slow and a bit awkward. Physically, you need to be able to reach your ankle easily and, the hard part, to be able to get back up in a hurry! When troops deployed from Ft. Bragg for Desert Shield and Desert Storm in the early nineties, ankle carry was popular for concealing an extra weapon. Soldiers were allowed to bring along personal firearms and knives discreetly tucked into boots as they boarded C-130 transport planes. This was especially popular with the women. Another occasion for ankle carry may be when formal clothing is required, and your shirt must be tucked.

Shoulder Carry.

This style carry brings the firearm up alongside one's rib cage by way of a cross-strap over the shoulders or a chest band and shoulder strap. Depending on the design of the holster, the weight of the firearm may be counterbalanced by an ammo pouch on the opposite side of the ribcage. A disadvantage of shoulder carry is the positioning—the muzzle of the gun is toward the rear with the grip forward. To draw, the user must reach across his/her chest and lift the firearm up and turn it forward. This presents the risk of a self-inflicted wound as well as a risk to friendlies in the vicinity. Added to this is the potential for a surprise attacker to reach for the gun. The shoulder carry position could not be any more perfect for a reach and grab.

Bra Carry, aka Miss Kitty Carry.

For women, there is a strap holster available that attaches over the center front of a conventional bra for CC. This and other forms of underwear carry are available. It looks uncomfortable. Ready access may be a problem. The big risk is a self-inflicted wound to the chest while drawing. I would *not* encourage this method of carry. Also, sweat is corrosive, not good for guns.

Pocket Carry.

This works well with deep pockets and loose-fitting clothes, traditionally, *a pant pocket.* Nothing else should be placed in the carry pocket, no keys, nothing else, only the gun inside a pocket holster on the dominant hand side, and always in a gun-specific holster. The holster serves as an extra safety. This is a great way to carry in a high-risk area. Hands in your pockets look relaxed and normal. Your hand will already be in contact with the firearm if it is needed. If you are using a jacket pocket, keep alert; removing the jacket may lead to a loss of the firearm, or worse.

Thigh Carry, or Garter Carry.

This style of holstering is made for wear with a dress or skirt, especially long formal wear. Adjustable garter holsters are available for approximately $50. Again, this is not a method of carry that I can highly encourage. The draw will be slow, it will require both hands, and it will cause you to take your eyes off the bad guy.

Motorcycle Carry.

For bikers engaged in concealed carry while traveling, the usual issues of comfort, concealability, and accessibility are extra challenging. The rider's position, forward leaning, upright, or reclining, will influence the carry method. Also, weather conditions, distance to the destination, and any planned stops at "gun free" locations will affect the method of carry.

Most riders choose some form of belt/holster carry, the same as they use every day. For long rides, a biker with CC license, may opt to carry a firearm in a tank bag that doesn't obstruct the view of gauges. The tank bag sits in front of the rider and is within easy reach for either hand. With any biker carry method, the smaller the firearm the easier the trip will be.

Stops along the way are a bit complicated. The rider should choose a carry method such that he or she can dismount without revealing the firearm. If "gun free" areas are on the itinerary, the biker is presented with the problem of where to store the handgun on the bike. Locks on biker bags may be an option, however flimsy. A hard metal or plastic saddle bag with a lock may provide some security. A hidden compartment with a lock would be ideal. Maybe some of the motorcycle makers will read this and respond.

In the unfortunate event of a tumble, it would be best to have the gun in a holster that is secured on the rider if the motorcyclist doesn't have a secure tank bag. If EMS gets involved, they should be advised that a gun had been with the rider, and they should help locate it. Bike riders should also carry pepper spray for lesser threats.

Purse and satchel carry for both men and women are discussed in Chapter 10, "A Word to Women".

OUR GUN-LOADED LANGUAGE

Shoot from the hip: means to respond quickly with little preparation or consideration. In reality, shooting from the hip may be the right thing when a rapid response to a threat is needed. Unlike the careful marksmanship involved in looking down the sites to line up the reticle and bead, a shot from the hip is hasty and depends on the shooter's hand eye coordination; shooting from the hip is only accurate in movies. The phrase is used to describe haphazard responses.

Holsters.

Quality holsters are a good investment; they make concealed carry much safer. My own experience with an inadequate holster made the point. I was driving with my holstered Glock 22. When I arrived at my destination and got out of my vehicle, I was startled by my loaded Glock falling to the ground in front of me, bouncing up, and pointing at my face ever so briefly. This gun was holstered at the beginning of my trip, but it had worked free as I traveled. Fortunately, the drop safety worked and there was no discharge. I invested in a better-made holster and have had no further problems.

An ideal holster should be comfortable, easily concealed, effective at keeping the firearm in place and it should make the draw easy. It should not cause pain or numbness. It is important to have the best available holster for your EDC (everyday carry) handgun. Holster selection is especially important in OWC.

Holsters today are more safely designed, usually from Kydex, a rigid molded plastic that prevents pressure inside the trigger guard. Most holsters are molded for a specific firearm. This should be considered at the time of purchase. Holsters are often sold together with the firearm to assure a good fit. Depending on the method of carry, the holster may be held in place by a belt clip or by belt pass-through slots. Some holsters are a combination of Kydex and leather. I don't recommend leather-only holsters because they can morph out of shape over time and impinge into the trigger zone. The holster for pocket carry needs to have an outside surface that drags or sticks inside of the pocket keeping the holster down. When you draw, you don't want the pocket holster coming out with the gun!

A sturdy gun belt is essential. These are available with polymer inserts, making them stronger for carrying a firearm. They are designed with leather over the inserts to give the appearance of an ordinary belt. Neoprene and nylon belts are available as well.

6

AUTOMATIC WEAPONS

Puckles's Patent

AN EARLY FORERUNNER OF AUTOMATIC WEAPONRY is known as the Puckle gun, patent 418, Old England, in 1718. The Puckle was brilliantly engineered and balanced, by James Puckle, who was also a lawyer and writer. His weapon depended on a flintlock firing mechanism which put a drag on its reliability. The huge, heavy, removable cylinder could hold (9) 32 mm rounds. On a good day with a good crew it could fire 63 bullets in seven minutes; that's 9 bullets per minute. It had the added benefit of alternating round bullets, useful "for shooting Christians", with square bullets, better suited for firing on "Muslim Turk pirates". Unfortunately for Puckle, the British Navy snubbed his invention. The Navy reckoned that it already had sailors who could fire three rounds per minute; if they mustered three of them together, the Puckle gun would become irrelevant. Only two Puckle guns were produced; one was sold to Duke John Montagu. (www.youtube.com, The Puckle gun: Repeating Firepower in 1718, 4NOV2021, Institute of Military Technology)

OUR GUN-LOADED LANGUAGE

Rapid-fire: an obvious reference to rapid gunfire as seen with a machine gun. The term is used to connote speed and energy. "Rapid fire" is used to describe any repeated action happening in quick succession, as in "rapid fire" interrogation.

"Automatic", "Full-auto", and "Machine" guns all mean the same thing. These are firearms that rapidly fire many rounds without manual reloading and are activated by a single pull of the trigger.

Surprisingly, federal law *does allow* a convoluted pathway for individual private ownership of these rapid-fire, repeat-action weapons. State laws may obstruct such purchases. The ATF closely regulates and taxes machine guns. Ryan Cleckner, writing for Rocket FFL, provides a guide through the complexities for anyone interested in owning a fully automatic weapon. (viewed 11OCT 2021Cleckner,R.'Who Can Own a Full-Auto Machine Gun? rocketffl.com/who-can-own-a-full-auto-machine-gun) Full-auto weapons have to be registered with the ATF, and are extremely expensive. Federal Law is unforgiving if machine gun violations happen, with penalties up to ten years prison, and up to $250,000 in fines. (Rose,V & Reilly, M 12JAN2009 SUMMARY OF STATE AND FEDERAL MACHINE GUN LAWS,cga.ct.gov/2009/rpt/2009-R-0020.htm) The rate of fire of these automatic weapons is reported to be 1100 rounds/minute, meaning it would consume eighteen rounds per second of trigger pull. Who could afford that?

An interesting example from this genre is the very rare Beretta 93R, a "true machine pistol", designed for the American CIA and the Italian anti-terrorism forces. It was only produced from 1979 to 1993. According to Larry Vickers of Vickers Tactical, the 93R has a fire selector right where the safety switch is located on other Berettas, so handle with discretion! The fire selector gives you two choices; switch up, for semi-automatic or switch down, for three-shot burst mode. It also features a detachable stock and an odd, retractable fore grip. We found this pistol IS available for purchase online for $45,000. Just click "ADD to CART". Shipping is free. Remember to get your NFA Stamps for $200 each! Two stamps may be required due to the butt stock and the select fire feature. (viewed 11 OCT2021, armsunlimited.com/Berette-93R-9mm-Machine-Pistol-p/93r.htm)

Notes on a Newly Purchased Firearm

New owners are eager to practice with a newly purchased firearm. Many go right out to a shooting venue and begin firing. This can be dangerous for the shooter because any obstruction in the barrel can interfere with proper function. Before beginning with a new firearm, or a new-to-you firearm, a bit of maintenance is in order. If your purchase is a previously owned gun, you should inspect and clean it thoroughly before use. Lightly lubricate it with gun oil per the instruction manual. For a new, never-used firearm, a quick cleaning, again, is in order. The new ones may have been treated with an anti-corrosive or preservative. This stuff can be hazardous to the shooter; it should be removed and gun oil applied as recommended. Do not assume it has been pre-lubricated.

I found this in *Instructions for Use of a Glock*: "…any obstruction in the barrel could … result in death or serious personal injury and/or damage to the pistol." Remove any residues by passing a cleaning patch through the barrel. Repeat until a cleaning patch comes out clean. Lightly lubricate the friction prone parts with gun oil to prolong the useful life of your firearm. Follow your owner's manual for cleaning instructions. If you feel unsure of this procedure, check with your seller's gunsmith to ask for a demo. So, there you have it, even Glock recommends cleaning and lubricating before shooting a new gun.

Remember when you transport a newly purchased gun in your vehicle, it's best to unload and pack it in a case for transport. This case should be stored in the uttermost part of your vehicle beyond your reach, the trunk of a car or the storage area in the back of an SUV. In a pick-up truck, store the case where it can be seen by law enforcement, should you be stopped.

7

SAFETIES
(AKA GUN SAFETY MECHANISMS)

THE SAFEST GUN IS ONE THAT fires when it should, and doesn't when it shouldn't. It seems so simple! A safety is a control feature that engages to prevent any unwanted shots coming from a firearm. A safety must easily disengage to allow firing. Early firearms had no safeties. Unexpected discharges from these early guns lead to development of a variety of safety mechanisms. Currently, with revolvers excepted, newer firearms may have one or multiple safeties. Most safeties are built into the firearms and don't require conscious manipulation by the user. This explains how we can collectively own more than 400 million guns in the United States and have relatively few unplanned shots fired. Often, gun owners are hardly aware of the safety features built into their weapons.

- A *trigger safety, also known as safe-action trigger* sits within the trigger guard, embedded with the trigger and provides a bit of impedance to the trigger squeeze. These can be seen on the Glock handguns.
- A *firing pin safety,* located inside the slide, stabilizes the firing pin until it is disengaged by the pull of the trigger.
- A *pistol grip safety or lemon squeezer* is a safety that keeps the pistol from firing, until the safety is switched off by a squeeze or firm grip on the pistol frame handle overlay. No squeeze, no gunfire. This grip safety, which acts as a drop safety as well, is a built-in feature that is hardly noticed by many shooters. Grip safeties are falling from favor because

the extra energy used to tighten the grip reduces the accuracy, if the shooter is under-trained, or has weak muscles as occurs in any of the muscular dystrophies.

- A *drop safety* should be renamed for clarity. It should be *gun-drop safety*. It is a mechanism that prevents firing when a gun is literally dropped. Remember the Westerns where the sheriff commands the bad guys to drop their guns? And they do just that. It was not such a great idea, considering the absence of drop safeties back in the day.

The various types of modern gun-drop safeties include: the firing pin block safety, the hammer block safety, the transfer bar, the manually engaged safety notch, and the pistol grip safety. Also, a custom holster protects the trigger area and serves as a safety as well. (Firearms History, Technology & Development Safety Mechanisms: Drop Safety 28JUL2011…armshistory.blogspot.com)

A *magazine disconnect mechanism* for a magazine loaded gun is another form of safety. Its purpose is to prevent the firing of a remaining chambered round when there is no magazine loaded into the magazine well. This is a requirement in California for all magazine-loaded handguns. (firearm related mortality and morbidity, JOHNS HOPKINS CENTER FOR GUN POLICY AND RESEARCH, giffords.org/lawcenter/gun-laws/policy-aread/child-consumer-safety/design-safety-standards/ viewed 26FEB2022)

A *loaded chamber indicator* tells the shooter, by feel, that there is a chambered round in the firearm. On a Glock pistol this is checked by feeling the position of the extractor. It sticks out when a round is chambered; it is recessed when the chamber is empty. This is not a true safety that blocks firing, but it helps the shooter know if a round is ready. It is helpful in the dark or when silence is needed.

A *decocker* is a lever that when depressed two things happen. The firing pin is blocked and the hammer is dropped to normal position or into a half-cock. This is useful during the night when you realize the "intruder" in your kitchen was just your ice maker.

A decocker is sometimes described as a safety, and sometimes as an alternative to a safety. The Beretta M9 is known for featuring a decocker. After being "decocked", the gun will be in a double-action setting which will allow firing with a heavier, longer trigger pull, so you are good to go if the intruder shows up after all. It depends on your definition whether this is a true safety. For those who worry about prompt reaction to an intruder, decockers are preferred over manual safeties. But you can have it both ways! Many double action semi-auto pistols have de-cockers and manual safeties. (Sam Hoober, 09AUG2017 *Decocker or Manual Safety: Which* https://legionary.com/decocker-vs-safety-which -is-better/)

OUR GUN-LOADED LANGUAGE

Locked and loaded: adv., hearkens to a military command to "Lock and load" or make ready for battle. Some purists argue that the sequence should be "load and lock". President Trump tweeted on August 11, 2017, that "Military solutions are now in place, locked and loaded, should North Korea act unwisely." Later in the day to those concerned as to how the North Koreans would interpret the phrase, he was quoted as saying, "Those words were very easy to understand." (Lin,H What Exactly Does 'Locked and Loaded mean? 15 AUG 2017lawfareblog. com)

The Great Debate about Manual Safeties

Manually operated safeties, aka "thumb" safeties, aka "external" safeties work like an ON-OFF switch and require user participation. This simple function is a huge point of contention for many who hold that, in a panicky moment of urgent need, the safety HAS TO BE in the OFF (disengaged) position. IF the thumb safety has been left ON (engaged), that needs to be corrected, before the gun will be useful, slowing down the response-to-threat time.

Conversely, if the thumb safety has been left OFF (disengaged) routinely, or the thumb safety does not exist on the firearm, there is risk of an unplanned shot being fired. Further complicating things, is the issue that thumb safeties are not standardized; that is, the up position may be ON for some firearms, and OFF for others.

"A safety can be very unsafe." – John Lovell. Lovell maintains that most gunfire exchanges are over in three seconds or less. The issue runs like this: 1) You are armed and minding your own business. 2) Suddenly, you perceive a threat, a bear, an armed bad guy—or a bad girl. 3) You think to draw your gun. 4) The threat persists as you take aim. 5) You pull the trigger and get a sick sounding click, no shot. 6) You diagnose the problem. The safety, you believe/hope, is the problem. 7) You take time to disengage the manual safety hoping your diagnosis is correct… Shaking, you try again to take aim… You are now in the twilight zone of what Lovell calls the "Three Second Mistake". At this point, your assailant will likely have the upper hand, and your battle is over. I tend to agree with Lovell.

It's easy to see why Lovell hates manual safeties. His YouTube rant goes on to state that the hard-side custom holsters, now available, serve as an adequate safety. He contends there is no need for a manual safety at all. Once the firearm comes out of the holster, you need it to be ready to go, according to this warrior. (*The PROBLEM with a Thumb Safety Pistol,* John Lovell, 20FEB2019 You Tube. WarriorPoetSociety.US)

The endless debate by Lovell and other YouTube giants comes down to this: is it better to risk the mistake of having a gun safety ON when you need it OFF, or do you chance having a gun go off unexpectedly for want of manual safety being ON? Despite our heritage of numerous firearm engineering geniuses, both scenarios still happen. It will be up to you to decide which is the greater risk for you and yours.

As previously mentioned, early handguns had no safeties. There were many occasions when a bump of the hammer resulted in disastrous live fire. Predictably, the Colt Single Action Army revolvers issued during the Civil War era, were a safety problem. Enterprising soldiers, however, resolved the issue by leaving one chamber of their six-cylinder revolvers empty. By rotating that empty cylinder to the position under the hammer, the problem was solved! This simple safety innovation can work even today for revolver owners. (Ben Findley 20FEB2015 *Handgun Safeties: Types and Characteristics* https://www.usacarry.com/handgun-safeties-types-characteristics/)

If you make a conscious decision to choose a firearm that has a manual safety, you need to practice manipulating the safety to the OFF position every time you bring the firearm up to shoot. Disengaging the safety should be well-rehearsed to develop muscle memory. US Military personnel have been using the Beretta M9, which features a manual safety. Before that, they were issued the legendary 1911, which featured a manual safety; today it appears they are gradually switching over to the Sig Sauer M17 as their service sidearm, again, with manual safety. This history lends support to the idea that a manual safety, with adequate training and instruction, is a reasonable choice.

8

AMMUNITION
AMMO, THE STUFF GOES POW AND PSCHEW PSCHEW!

WITHOUT AMMO, GUNS GROW QUIET AS security becomes an issue in all sectors; and, the entire annual $63.5B firearms industry grinds to a halt. (Economic Impact of Gun Industry Up 232% since '08,3/18/2021by National Shooting Sports Foundation game-andfishmag.com) The most frequent question I am asked about ammunition is, "What about the shortage?" There is a shortage of ammo, and many retailers are rationing. A shortage began during the Obama administration with panic buying related to the *threat* of governmental gun grabbing. Supplies and pricing improved until the emergence of the Covid crisis during the winter of 2019-2020, and shortages returned. The current shortage has caused cancellation or curbing of shooting classes, sport shooting events, and even police training. (9/13/21,COVID-19,politics to blame for ammunition shortage…The Spokesman-Review) Though the situation has improved a bit, we still have shortages, particularly of the .380 ACP caliber, a slightly smaller diameter than 9 mm (.355 inches) sometimes referred to simply as 380s. These are popular for use in the smaller handguns used for concealed carry. Other calibers are in short supply as well, but there seems to be a design to the .380 (.380 ACP) shortage. Ammo manufacturers are converting some die machinery to favor the production of the 9mm round, a larger, more widely used caliber, as they cut back on production of 380s. Supposedly, this is to meet the demands of uniformed services. Industry insiders predict the shortage will go on for two years. Mike Furrer, a competitive shooter and coach from Spokane, states, "The current shortage … is the worst I've ever seen." (9/13/21,COVID-19,politics to blame for ammunition shortage…The Spokesman Review.) Most analysts attribute the shortage to increased demand. With each gun sale, one or two boxes of five to100 rounds of ammo usually go out as well. With 37 million recent gun sales, that comes to a conservative estimate of 2 billion ammo units. I'm thinking our problem is simple; demand outpaces supply. The shortage is unfortunate in that many new gun owners may not be able to get the hands-on live-fire training and practice needed to become proficient.

While I encourage gun owners to maintain adequate supplies of ammo, I am opposed to the purchase of ammo for resale purposes. If you buy ammo beyond the amount you can responsibly manage or use, you might be hurting someone else's ability to train and/or defend. Consider: 1) Hoarding drives prices higher. 2) The loss in supply may impact hands-on training for professionals, as well as civilian gun owners. A lack of training increases unwanted incidents. 3) Storage of excessive ammo supplies may pose a risk to you, your family and to first responders. Take into consideration that in the event of a home fire, exploding ammo will complicate rescue and containment. 4) Improperly stored ammo deteriorates and becomes hazardous and useless.

Saving Ammo through Techno-Target Practice

You probably never dreamed that a bit of electronic technology would find its way down the chamber of that old Luger P.08 that your great-grandfather brought home from the war. Brace yourself! It's here!

Some companies are now marketing practice shooting systems. These feature *electronic* cartridges that, when fired, flash a laser onto an ordinary target. It is amazing that a laser apparatus could be miniaturized to fit into the space normally occupied by a conventional cartridge! Using an app downloaded to your phone, these systems are able to watch as you shoot and record the placement of the laser flashes on the target. You get a visual image on your screen showing your grouping accuracy. These electronic cartridges come in various sizes, compatible with commonly used calibers. They essentially convert your practice firearm to a laser gun, while allowing the normal maneuvers of practice firing. It is recommended that all real ammo be removed from the practice area. "Always remember to follow all gun safety rules at all times." Caution must be taken that the laser is never flashed into anyone's eyes. The space should be free of excess ambient light that will interfere with the laser image on the target. It will be a bit weird at first, to fire a real gun indoors, but these systems are promoted as a practice alternative that can be used at home, while saving countless rounds of ammo. While this system can be useful, live-fire practice will still be advisable. Just as in dryfire practice, the user of this type system will miss the recoil experience. Another drawback is that many gun owners will avoid anything that has even a slight potential for surveillance. Yet, reviews have been favorable. (g-sight.com/products/slms-plus-laser-trainingsystem40w?currency=USD&variant=39817364111471&utm_medium=cpc&utm_source=google) There are many similar systems available. This review is not meant to endorse one system over any other.

Storage for Your Ammo

Before you bring home your ammo, you need a plan for storage. Get the opinion of your local firefighter. Counterintuitive, yet, the most expensive steel storage container may not be the optimal choice. In the event of a very hot fire, those military style, sealed, steel storage boxes may cause all the ammo units stored in them to heat and explode simultaneously. When this happens, the metal container explodes into "dangerous bits of shrapnel, in addition to [flying] bullets and casings". (How Dangerous is Ammunition in a House Fire by David Maccar 5/16/2017RANGE LIFE) The usual alternative to a metal storage box is a hard plastic polymer container. As any Cub Scout can tell you, burning plastics give off extremely toxic fumes. Therefore, the firefighters' advice to use a *wooden* storage box makes sense. The article continues: a) Ammo should be routinely stored in a wooden box. b) In case of an active fire, if possible, ammo and firearms should be removed from the burning structure. If you do home fire drills with your family, removing the firearms and ammo should be part of the drill. Currently, I can only find one supplier of wooden ammo boxes. That is Alta Max LLC of New Orleans, LA. On another note, do you know a talented woodworker who has a heart for first responders? These wooden ammo boxes could even be sold as fundraisers to support firefighters!

Maccar's article goes on to explain that in a burning structure, a loaded firearm may pose an even greater threat than boxed ammo. Heated ammo "cooking off" in a firearm is the same as if someone pulled the trigger; the pressure buildup in the barrel accelerates the round just as it is designed to do, creating an even greater risk to first responders.

Storing your ammo in a separate location from your firearms is highly recommended for obvious reasons; and conversely, keeping them together can be argued as well. Unused guns should definitely be stored separate from their ammo. Those in the separate-storage camp are thinking of children and others who might accidentally, or intentionally, chamber and discharge a round. Some states, as of this writing, require separate storage by law. These include Massachusetts, Connecticut, California, and New York. (Why Should You Store Ammo and Guns Separately? 9/22/21protectandlock.com/store-ammo-guns-separately) For your bug-out gun , the one you grab in an emergency evacuation, your home-defense long gun, and your concealed carry pistol, with the correct ammo, should be conveniently hidden, readily available, or even loaded into the firearm, *provided that only you, the gun owner have quick, easy access.* Conversely, if there is any risk that a child, or mentally unstable adult, or a thief might get access to your guns and ammo, you are legally responsible. Don't let that happen! You can be found guilty of negligence if you fail to secure your firearms and/or ammo away from those who should not have them.

Long term storage of Ammo.

As supply lines become less reliable, and prices increase, ammunition that you have on hand becomes more critical. Having a plan for long-term storage is wise. Your supply should be protected from friction or jostling, from extremes of heat and cold, and from dampness. Using a vacuum seal with a silica pack inside is one option to protect your ammo from corrosion. You can use a simple vacuum sealer like the ones sold for vacuum sealing food. Wear gloves to keep oil from your fingers off the casings. Silica packs can be ordered online. Be sure to label each package with date and caliber. It is a good idea to flatten and tape the original cartridge box to the vacuum sealed package before storing it in your safe.

Ammo Origins.

Once upon a time, back a thousand years or so, and probably in China, somebody confined potassium nitrate (saltpeter), charcoal, and sulfur in a closed space and supplied a spark. Boom! Black powder! Celebrations would never be the same, and neither would warfare. Shortly afterward, black powder was packed into bamboo tubes and the distal end was loaded with rocks. Upon ignition, we had the first ever projected ammo; the concept was born. Moving into the fifteenth century the projected ammo took the form of lead balls. Lead spheres and cones were cast for firearms, and loaded into primitive weapons. (viewed 9/21/21shop. otmtactical.com/The-history-of-Ammunition-The-First-Bullet)

OUR GUN-LOADED LANGUAGE

Here's the story of Guy Fawkes. He must have thought black powder, in good quantity, was sufficient. Why bother with a firearm?

The Guy with the Gunpowder

When was the last time you said, "You guys!" or "Wise Guy"? Or, if you are from the Boston area, perhaps it was "Yous Guys!" Point of order: you only say "Yous Guys" loudly, with emphasis. "Yous" should be divided into two syllables, "You-oous Guys!" Would you believe the expression has existed for more than 400 years? Did you ever think it might have had anything to do with a real person and with gunpowder?

The original "Guy" was an ambitious fellow named Guy Fawkes. He was found hiding in the cellar of the British Parliament building on the night of November 4, 1605. He had prepared thirty-six barrels of gunpowder down there for detonation. His intent was to annihilate King James I and the entire House of Parliament as they were opening the session on the following morning. Fortunately, for the King, and the Lords, the plot was discovered around midnight, well ahead of the legislative session. After his arrest, Guy Fawkes was persuaded by way of torture to expose his accomplices. He was sentenced to hanging despite having cooperated with authorities. On his way up the ladder to the gallows, he jumped, fell, broke his neck, and died.

The following year on November 5th, all of England celebrated "Guy Fawkes Night" burning effigies of Guy Fawkes and giving thanks that his plot had been foiled. (www.history.com/topics/british-history/ gunpowder-plot, viewed 4NOV2021) From that time on, anyone who dressed crudely or had a rumpled appearance resembling the crude Guy Fawks effigies became known as a "Guy"! The gunpowder plot even became the inspiration for a release by John Lennon of the Beatles in 1969, called "Remember". And that's the story of how "You GUYS," living in the twenty-first century, came about.

Crude Beginnings to Mind-Blowing Capacity!

More than 300 years ago, the oldest known true firearm on earth, the muzzle-loading rifle, gave this black powder concoction an expanded role. Primitive by today's standards, the force generated by igniting black powder behind a bullet inside a narrow barrel was an astounding development. Initially used for sport and hunting, the muzzle-loader rapidly became the choice weapon of war. Muzzle loaders were prized by the likes of King Louis XIII of France, Napoleon Bonaparte, and George Washington.

In 1807, Rev. Alexander Forsyth of Scotland, who understood the importance of keeping his powder dry, patented a system for keeping the black powder inside the gun. His idea developed as the result of a disappointing hunting trip during foul weather. This was yet another concept that contributed to the gradual development of today's ammo. (McClintock,B,11FEB2011popularmechanics.com/military/weapons/g514/the-modernization-of-the-muddleloaded-rifle/)

Fortunately, the tedious process of muzzle-loading lasted for a few centuries, which surely slowed the pace of war, globally.

In the mid-1800s, breech-loading handguns and rifles appeared, making reloading faster and easier. With these, the load materials were chambered behind the barrel, which later led to the adoption of packaged ammo in the form of a cartridge that contained all the essentials. Later, things became yet more efficient with the development of arms that automatically ejected the spent shell. This helped speed the reloading process.

Over time, we learned to reload faster and faster, until now, in the twenty-first century, we have the Australian-made Metal Storm Gun that reportedly, fires at the rate of 1 million rounds per minute. There is no time for chemicals and cartridges with this busy piece of hardware. It only wants the bullets, all fired electronically. (Adarsh Verma 17FEB2016 *Watch How the World's Fastest Gun Fires 1 Million Rounds Per Minute* FossBytes-Gadgets&Machinefossbytes.com)

The Controlled Burn within Cartridges

A unit of rifle or handgun ammo is properly referred to as a *cartridge.* How can a simple cartridge punch out a bear? To answer this, we consider the anatomy and the chemistry of a cartridge. A *cartridge* is an assembly of component parts including a casing, a primer, a measured quantity of gunpowder, and a bullet protruding out of the leading end. Think of the *casing* as a small canister that holds everything in place, designed to fit inside the chamber of a same-caliber firearm. Cartridge casings may be tapered to optimize ballistics. The casing is almost always made of a brass alloy, though aluminum, plastic, and even paper have been tried. Stamped on the base of a cartridge, you will find the caliber and the maker's name. For safety, you should always meticulously match the recommended cartridge(s) to your specific firearm.

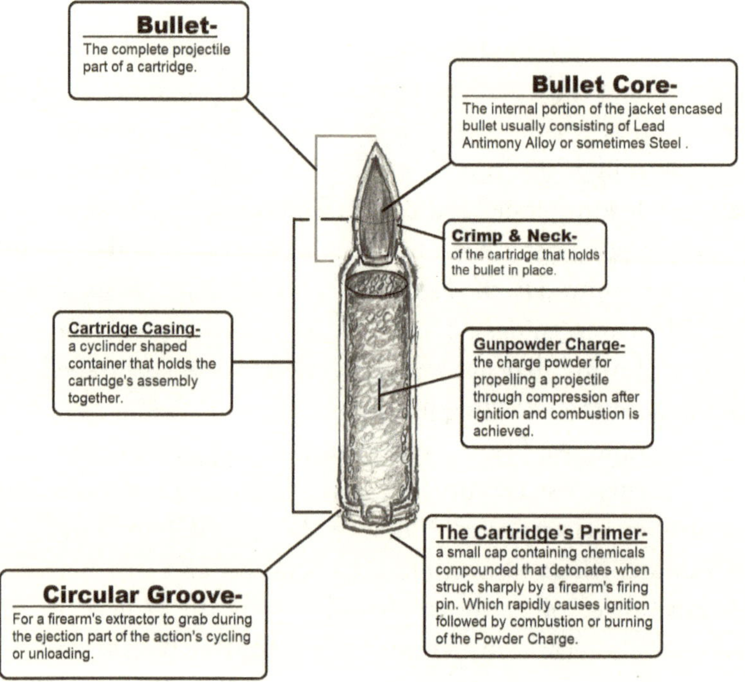

Cartridge Cutaway

The *primer*, located in the base of the cartridge, receives the impact of the firing pin. The primer consists of a small metal alloy cup containing a minute amount of an amber-colored crystalline substance called an impact-ignited lead styphnate (say stiff'n-eight), aka lead azide. This highly explosive, impact sensitive, chemical, has molecules that are loaded with oxygen atoms, enabling it to burn without air!

The primer is contained in the rim of the casing in rim-fire cartridges and in the center of the cartridge base in center-fire cartridges. Your firearm is configured for either, but not both. The firing pin strikes the primer on center, or on some point on the rim of the base, depending on the type of firearm-ammo combination you are using. The sequence is: 1) The firing pin hits the primer, delivering pressure. 2) The impact sensitive igniter in the primer explodes first and ignites the gunpowder, aka propellant, inside the casing. 3) The gunpowder, which can be black powder, or nitro-cellulose, the smokeless (note that is "less" smoke, not smoke free) gun powder, ignites to a rapid controlled burn. 4) Heat builds up instantly causing gasses in the cartridge to expand and create pressure. 5) The rising pressure inside the cartridge forces the bullet off its perch, releasing the bullet and the expanding gasses into the barrel, where the force increases the bullet's velocity and propels it out of the muzzle. 6) By the time the bullet leaves the muzzle, it has absorbed enough energy to resist gravity and continue at speeds of up to 2600 ft./sec, rifle speed, twice the speed of sound; that is 1800 miles per hour! ([Raw Materials, madehow.com/Volume-2/Ammunition, viewed 18OCT 2021] and [How Fast Can a Bullet Travel, wonderopolis.org, viewed 20 OCT 2021])

If at any point along the way, a cartridge misfire or other incident should happen, it will be helpful to have the package information, so you should keep cartridge packaging until the contents are expended. The manufacturer will want the lot number. Recalls of ammunition have happened.

It's All About the Bullets

OUR GUN-LOADED LANGUAGE

Sweating bullets: to be very nervous and worried. (www.Merriam-webster.com viewed 30 Oct 2021) The origins of this expression are obscure, but most likely, it is connected to the shot tower process of dropping liquid molten lead through a chimney into a container of water to form lead shot, aka bullets, during the muzzle loader era. It must have been a demanding, hot, sweat producing, intensive job during wartime.

The term, *bullet(s)*, is often used for ammunition in general. This likely originated with the chief responsibility of Army logistics, to procure and distribute ample supplies of *bullets and beans*. However, this loose use of the word has contributed to some confusion. Only in muzzle loading, is the bullet a separate item, loaded separately, following the gunpowder and a greased wad or patch. A unit of rifle or handgun ammo is composed of a *cartridge,* or *round,* having the bullet encased in the forward portion.

The relatively small bullet portion is destined to exit the cartridge assembly and the firearm barrel, to travel to the target, leaving the casing behind. The speed can vary, depending on a variety of factors.

Most bullets are made of lead and have an electroplated copper or other metallic coating, called a full metal jacket (FMJ), which blocks corrosion and adds strength, and oddly, the metal jacket reduces stopping power. I was amused during the Rittenhouse trial when the prosecutor described with great emphasis that the ammo used in the incident was *"FULL METAL JACKET!"* He implied that FMJ meant increased lethality. Quite the opposite is true. Perhaps he was assuming ignorance on the part of the jury; or, maybe he just didn't know. The metal jacket tends to keep the lead core together on impact, reducing the damage to the target.

An important characteristic of a bullet is the weight or mass which is measured in grains (gr.). The grain weight may range from fifteen to 750 grains and the value may vary even as the caliber of a unit of ammo stays the same. For reference, a dime coin weighs approximately thirty-five grains. Bullet grain weight is usually printed on the packaging. This value is one clue to how the bullet will perform. The lighter a bullet, the faster it will travel when propelled by an equivalent force. However, the lighter grain weight bullets can be blown off target by wind. Conversely, heavier bullets move out more slowly but travel with less wind interference and they are less affected by turbulence. (Baker,C.Choosing theRightBulletWeighthttps://www.luckygunner.com/lounge/chooding-the-right-bullet-weight/)

The shape of the bullet will contribute to its performance. Most have a rounded, cone shaped tip for decreased drag. A lead bullet with a full alloy coating, or FMJ (full metal jacket), with its rounded tip and decreased drag, is less expensive to produce. These are more economical for practice. For self-defense, round tipped, or RN for "round nose", cartridges are frowned upon as they are likely to pass right through soft tissues of a live target and fail to stop the offender. Another criticism is that a rounded FMJ bullet is more likely to continue through and beyond a target, inflicting unintended injuries.

Bullets that Morph on Impact, Game Changers

From the first World War, there arose complaints that the British and French were using soft, exposed lead bullets and/or drilled out (hollow-point) bullets. The effect of the "soft" dome of the bullet was to allow alteration of the shape of the bullet on impact. This loss of symmetry caused tumbling as the lead blob entered soft tissue, thus expanding the wound tract. The effect was like that of a much larger caliber shot. These projectiles became known as "Dum-Dum Bullets" for the town in India, Dum-Dum, where they were produced. Despite having been banned by Article 23 of the Hague Convention(s), of 1899 and 1907, there were wide-spread reports of the use of Dum-Dum-Geschosse (German for Dum-Dum bullets) across the war theater. (*The Soldier at the Western Front- The Use of Dum-DumProjectiles*www.hi.uni-stuttgart.de/wgt/ww-one/Start/Bleed_White/Technology_and_Science/ww1_ger_08_05. Html)

Hollow-point bullets are widely used for law enforcement and home defense in the US, despite the ban on their use in warfare by the Hague Declaration and the Geneva Convention. Hollow-points are banned in the State of New Jersey, with exceptions. These bullets were designed to expand on impact, causing greater disruption inside the target, and a wider wound track, resulting in increased lethality. (nytimes.com/1997/03/07/opinion/hold-off-on-hollow-point-bullets, viewed 16 OCT2021) Hollow-point bullets mushroom out on impact and stop rapidly after penetrating the target. This delivers more energy where it is intended, while reducing exit issues and unintended injury to by-standers. An exploded hollow-point generally stays in one piece as the tip fans out a little like a flower opening. For these reasons, hollow points are widely recognized as a better product for self-defense. They are easily identified by a tiny scooped out crater in the tip. Also, the soft metal of the core is exposed by way of a "well" down through the core of the bullet. (gunbelts.com/blog/all-about-hollow-point-bullets, viewed 16 OCT2021) This allows a flowering effect of the core contents on impact, delivers more force to the internal organs, and cuts a wider diameter tract of injury. Translation: more stopping power. This design is significantly more lethal when compared to the penetration of an FMJ cone or tapered bullet. Some people hesitate when they understand that hollow-points are more deadly. My thought is that when the threat is clear, it is important to stop the assailant as quickly as possible without the risk of pass-through damage beyond the target. In dealing with a real threat, you need specific defensive loads that are effective, not sloppy.

*(I am aware of artsy types using spent hollow point 'flowers' to make jewelry. I don't advise this. You don't need the lead exposure.

The *Radically Invasive Projectile (RIP)* is next in the progression of lethal ammo. "It is well named. The RIP Bullet is designed to create massive wounding, leading to rapid blood loss and target incapacitation." – Kyle Mizokami.

The RIP tip is defined by a group of eight pointed copper members that form a crown over an open core down to the solid bullet base. Its machine-like action is new in two ways. First, it is like a drill as the spinning pointed crown burrows into the target.

Next, on impact, the pointed copper fragments, trocars, symmetrically break apart and fan out, reminiscent of fireworks in a night sky. The RIP creates eight divergent wound channels followed by the wound tract of the larger, trailing, bullet base, for a total of nine wound tracts. It causes fragmenting cavitation upon penetration and impact. The effect is achieved through outward pressure on the trocars as the hollow portion of the bullet fills with the soft tissue of the target. These cartridges are powered to the level that they can easily penetrate auto glass, sheetrock, sheet metal, multiple layers of denim, and of course human or animal tissue. The design is being adapted for a variety of calibers of handguns, long guns, and for shotgun slugs as well. (*The Next Step in the Bullet Evolution,* 2016 Royal Content, You Tube www.GR2Ammo) I question the use of this one for putting meat on the table. It might be hard to get all those scattered trocars out of the product.

The good news: RIP Bullets contain no lead, which makes them, ironically, a bit kinder to the environment. (Kyle Mizokami *Introducing the RIP Bullet: The Most Dangerous Ammo You Can Legally Buy?* 03Jan2019 The NationalInterestnationalinterest.org.)

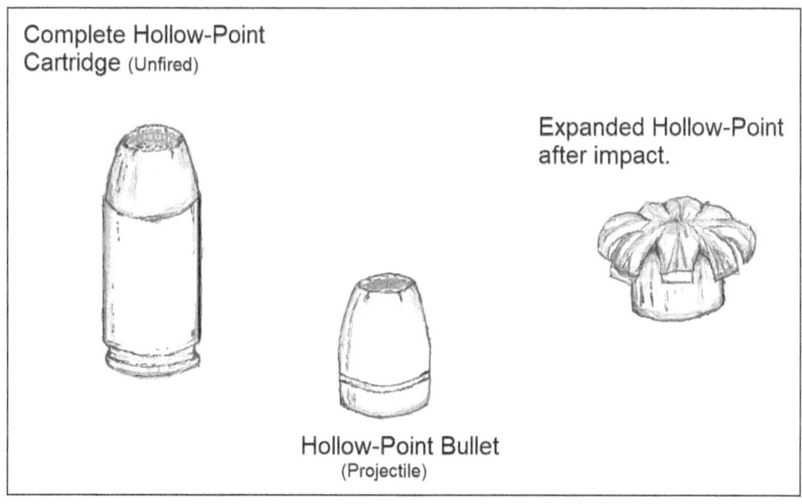

Less Lethal Ammo?

Frangible Bullets

While hollow-point bullets morph into a mushroom shape, and RIPs send out lethal shards on impact, *frangible bullets* (SinterFire, Inc.) disintegrate entirely to form fine particles and copper dust when they hit hard targets. Frangible bullets penetrate poorly but can cause serious superficial damage. Frangibles are helpful in close-quarter training exercises, where both over-penetration and ricochet pose hazards to property or personnel. These also work well where there are other environmental concerns such as elements of infrastructure, or tanks nearby, or rocky terrain that might cause ricochet.

An argument could be made for using frangible ammo for home defense, when the home is part of a multi-family unit and a stray bullet through a wall could be disastrous. Assuming the home-defense firearm is only fired rarely, the frangible ammo would be an acceptable choice. For pests, frangible bullets perform well against soft targets such as coyotes.

A cool fact about frangible bullets is that they are lead free, mostly made of copper. After firing, the residual powder is harmless to the environment. This may be one answer to concerns for setting up an outdoor firing range.

The downside to frangible bullets is that they penetrate poorly, leaving nasty superficial wounds. The disintegrating particles may cause barrel damage to the firearm faster than conventional bullets. When shooting frangible bullets, you will need to clean your gun more frequently. With high frequency of use, the residual powder becomes messy. (ammunitiontogo.com/lodge/what-is-frangible-ammo/ viewed 07JAN22)

"Rubber" bullets, aka Kinetic Impact Projectiles (KIPs).

For starters, rubber bullets are not necessarily made of rubber, and they are not non-lethal. There is no standardization of what constitutes a rubber bullet. They may be composed of metal, plastic, or wood, usually with a thin, rubberized outer layer. The injuries from the use of rubber bullets, KIPs, tend toward non-penetrating contusions and bruising; however, an array of significant injuries and deaths have been reported. Historically, they have been employed by law enforcers for riot control.

Kaiser Health News along with *USA Today* reported an unarmed non-threatening graduate student lost an eye due to a plastic-tipped round, aka "rubber bullet", being fired at him during the George Floyd protests in Minnesota. (Dennis Wagner , *Minneapolis Police Injured Protesters With Rubber Bullets. The City Has Taken Little Action.* June 2021, USA Today, KHN.org.) A host of other injuries have been reported over many years, including brain injury, disfiguring facial injuries, fractures, nerve injuries, and penetrating injuries to internal organs.

A report from the United Nations states that KIPs should only be directed toward the lower body, never toward the face, head, or neck. This is a problem because KIPs tend to go off course due to the irregular shape, which contributes to unintended injuries. (Rubber Bullets can be deadly, expersts say, as George Floyd protests put spotlight on police use of the projectiles, by Ayodola Aidgun and Eden David 09JUN2020, abcnews.go.com)

"Bean Bag Rounds", hardly harmless.
Generally, these are non-penetrating to a target. Bean Bag rounds can fracture a skull, fracture neck spines, rupture eyeballs, interfere with heart and lung function, and cause internal bleeding. Bean Bags are not recommended for home defense due to unreliable stopping capability. (*Are Bean Bag Rounds for Home Defense a Good Idea?* Evan Graham)

Another Supposed Non-lethal Projectile.
As of 2022, "the Byrna", an interesting concept mentioned on the nighttime TV show "Hannity", is being advertised as a "non-lethal" (?) option for self-defense. Reportedly, it is available with no waiting period and no background checks. By using CO2 cartridges, his product "launches", not "fires" a variety of projectiles.

These include "Eco-kinetic" spherical projectiles, pepper-spray/tear gas projectiles, pepper spray with synthetic projectiles, and other spherical "projectiles" made of hard solid plastic. Despite appearances, the advertiser is careful not to use words common in the firearms industry, like "gun", "ammo", and "firing". In my opinion, this "launching" device looks a lot like a typical handgun silhouette with a grip, barrel, trigger guard and trigger. This system is touted as a "game changer" available by simple mail order.

I am conflicted about this product. I can envision some applications where this would be brilliant. I am glad that non-lethal defense innovation is developing. I would always encourage that, because an every-day carry system is needed. My concern for this system is the handgun-like appearance that may be confused by, say, an officer at a traffic stop, or others in defensive situations. Remember an officer will have data based on a car's license tag, that may put him or her on high alert. I can envision the product being perceived as a gun, drawing return fire in a tense situation, despite its optional bright colors. My thought is that only a real gun should look like a gun. Do your own research on this product and form your own opinion. (*Byrna.com, viewed. 08 AUG 2022*)

What About Blanks?

Surely, blanks are harmless, right? Well, yes and no. Blanks are formed of cartridges and propellant (gunpowder), but only a paper or plastic wad instead of the bullet or shot. Except for ear damage caused by close-range loud noise, anything two feet or more away from the blast should be safe. Blanks are sometimes loaded with extra propellant to get a louder bang. Blanks fired from a gun placed to the head have caused self-inflicted skull fractures and death. Blanks can be fired from ordinary firearms, but they are usually fired using special blank guns. (*CAN YOU SHOOT BLANKS IN A REAL GUN, Hunting heart/By Tobias huntingheart. com/can-you-shoot-blanks-in-a-real-gun/ viewed 01APR2022*)

The use of less-than-lethal defensive devices is fraught with unintended episodes of real damage to a target. The diminished stopping power of less than lethal options may come with unintended consequences, in that an assailant may be recast as the victim, upon review of the occurrence. An old adage goes, "Never bring a knife to a gunfight." Perhaps this thought should apply to less than lethal defense methods as well. However, every situation is different. Use your best judgment, training, and knowledge.

.22s, The Most Popular Cartridges

.22s are cartridges that have been around the States since they were introduced in America, in 1857, by Smith & Wesson. They are less expensive than other cartridges, and they are a bit less noisy with a gentler kick. .22s are too light for big game hunting, but they perform well for small game and target sports. They can be used in a variety of handguns, revolvers, and rifles. Be careful though. Not all .22s are the same. I have found seven different types of .22s. The .22 short, the .22 Long Rifle (LR), the .22 Magnum, the .22 Long, the .22 Flobert, which is described as a BB cap for antique guns, the .22 Winchester Rimfire, and the .22 TCM.

The .22 ammo that's most in demand, currently, is the .22 Long Rifle, or .22 LR, not to be confused with the .22 Long. The .22 LR has a heavier bullet and it packs more propellant than the .22 Long. The velocity is a respectable 1200 ft./sec. or more. The .22 LRs are in demand for most of today's semi-automatic handguns and rifles. Acmen.com explains that in yet other iterations of .22 LRs, you will find LRN (lead round nose) and CPRN (copper plated round nose) a super-high velocity, 40-grain bullet with a copper-plated round nose; and another CPRN, a bit lighter, at 34-grains bullet weight, advertised as having the ability to travel 1500 ft./sec. (acmen.com/best-places-to-buy , viewed 23 OCT 2021)

The .22 Winchester Magnum Rimfire (WMR) is a heavier, more powerful cartridge than traditional .22s. The word "magnum" implies greater power. It is an alternative to heavier defensive loads that deliver an excessive recoil. A drawback to the WMR, though it is classed as a .22, it has a casing that is too large for the chamber of a traditional bore .22-Caliber firearm. Firearms that have been developed to accommodate the very effective .22 WMR, include bolt-action and semi-automatic rifles, as well as handguns made by Ruger, Charter Arms, Kel-Tec, Smith & Wesson, Rock Island Armory (producer of the M1911 A1 XT), and North American Arms. (8 Top Choices for Handguns, wideopenspaces.com viewed 1 Nov. 2021)

9mm, The Go-to for Self Defense – Not for the Frail

The 9mm stands out as the go-to round for police work. An extensive FBI study from the late '80s concluded that 9mm rounds are best for law enforcement; "… it allows more rounds in the handgun. It has less recoil, is less expensive, and its penetration compares favorably with larger-sized rounds. It enables struggling shooters to attain better weapon control/shot placement and permits skilled shooters to be faster and more accurate." (Callahan, M., why bullet size matters in officer-involved shootings,police2. com, viewed 1 Nov. 2021) Some highly recommended 9mm handguns include the 9mm Luger introduced in 1901, the Glock 19, the Sig P226, and the Smith & Wesson M&P 9. (Mizokami,K. Say Hello to the 5 Best 9mm Guns on the Planet.nationalinterest. org, viewed 1NOV2021)

The 5.7x28 Caliber

FN was the first to develop the 5.7x28 caliber for military use to better penetrate body armor. Testing has proven this caliber to be superior to 9x19mm cartridges. It has become a standard for numerous military and police operations, including the US Secret Service. It is a small but powerful caliber that works well for selected concealable handguns. It is sold in six variations including a frangible and a blank. (Ortiz, Miguel, March,23,2022, *How NATO standardized the FN 5.7x28mm cartridge* wearethemighty.com) The 5.7x28 caliber is light weight at 27-grains. It is a high velocity, flat shooting, low recoil cartridge recommended for concealed carry firearms produced by FN, Ruger, Kel-Tec, AR Five-Seven, and the CMMG Banshee. This caliber is for self-defense. It is not a big game stopper.

Shotgun Ammo

Shotguns require shotgun shells which are loaded with pellets or slugs most commonly. Pellet-loaded shells produce a spray effect within a relatively shorter range than bullets. Shotgun pellet spray distance is highly variable, with rough estimates at twenty to 100 yards. Shell packages usually show the expected velocity rather than a measure of propellant. The pellets packed into shotgun shells vary in size and material used, depending on the desired effect. Common shell sizes are 12-gauge and 20-gauge. Less common sizes include .410 and 16-gauge.

Hazard Warning – Keep 20-Gauge shells OUT of your 12-Gauge!

20-gauge shells are color coded YELLOW as a safety measure. The yellow color is a warning to NEVER LOAD a 20-gauge shell into a 12-gauge shotgun. Remember the higher the gauge, the smaller the shell. A 20-gauge shell is small enough to disappear down the barrel of a 12-gauge and stick in the forcing cone. This leaves space for a second shell, a 12-gauge to be loaded by an ill-fated sportsman. If the gun is fired with this double load, possibly, the 20-gauge shell will blow out the end of the barrel in the right direction. However, there is also the possibility of a retrograde explosion, that can result in serious upper body injury to the shooter, and/or destruction of the shotgun's mechanism.

Implausible as it may seem, this scenario happens with some regularity. It has been recommended that 20-gauge shells be kept entirely away from 12-gauge shotguns to prevent someone absentmindedly dropping in a smaller shell and later following it with a larger one.

Shotgun shells are sometimes identified as "high brass" or "low brass", referring to the height of the brass, or aluminum, base of the shell. High Brass is not necessarily more powerful or more accurate, though it is more expensive. (Gregg Elliott, *What You Should Know About Shotgun Shells,* March 7. 2018 PROJECTUPLAND.COM/ AUTHOR/DOGSANDDOUBLES/)

An interesting shotgun shell is known as Dragon's Breath, which is packed with magnesium pellets. This shell creates sparks and flames out to approximately 100 feet. The fire hazard with this ordinance should be obvious. Another form of ammo for use with a shotgun for big game is the slug. A slug consists of a single, large, heavy bullet shell. The materials used for this may be metals, some plastics, and even rubber; the metal ones being the most lethal. There are even reports of shotgun shells being loaded with rock salt. This load may cause injury at close range, however, down range, rock salt is ineffective. Rock salt can damage the shotgun barrel, if not cleaned immediately.

Novelty Ammo

Hard-metal bullets, made from metals like steel, tungsten, brass, bronze or even depleted uranium (desirable for its density or weight) and are larger than .22 caliber, are known as *armor-piercing bullets*; these are regulated under 18 U.S.C. 921(a)(17) (c). (NotArmorPiercing-ButlerEagle,butlereagle.com, viewed 16OCT2021)

Green Tip M855 and M193 rounds, while not classified as armor piercing, are thought to match military grade ammo. These are good, inexpensive, all-around cartridges, distinguished by green paint on the tip of the pointy bullet. The *boat tail* feature of these simply means the projectile bullet tapers a bit to the rear, which improves speed, delivering greater energy to the target. (viewed on 16 OCT 2021,Jones,A, GreenTipM855vs. M193Ammo,ammunitiontogo.com/lodge/m855-vs-m193/)

Subsonic ammunition. Just as the name implies, these bullets travel slower than the speed of sound. Subsonic is often used with a suppressor (See "Choosing the right bullet weight.")

Flat Nosed bullets are used for precision target shooting. A favorite of exhibition shooters, flat nosed bullets produce a crisp punch-out of a target.

Tracer rounds. These are rounds loaded with a magnesium/strontium combination along with chlorine to keep things cool. Their purpose is to provide a brief flash of white light over the field of fire. Tracers were developed over a hundred years ago to expose an enemy's position. Unfortunately, they also revealed the shooter's position more accurately. Later iterations of tracers held off lighting the sky until they were 100 yards from the shooter. These were known as "subdued". Before you order, bear in mind that tracers are classified as explosives and the ATF requires that handlers are licensed to possess the same. Unauthorized possession is a felony. Also, there may be state and local ordinances, so, be aware. (*What are Tracer Rounds and Are They Legal?*ammoforsale.com/ammo-club/what-are-tracer-rounds-and-are-they-legal?/viewed 30MAR2022)

Requirements for Purchase of a Firearm

Requirements vary state to state and laws and rulings change constantly. Therefore, you will need to be up on the situation at the site of your purchase and interstate laws as well if you plan to travel with a firearm. The following are some guidelines as they exist currently in my area.

The requirements for a gun purchase include factors such as age greater than eighteen years old to purchase a rifle, and age greater than twenty-one years old, to purchase a pistol. An applicant must be free of any criminal history, as revealed by the National Instant Criminal Background Check System, aka NICS. This is under the auspices of the FBI. Known violent felons in the US are prohibited from gun ownership for life. However, we must bear in mind that lawbreakers frequently acquire firearms, regardless of legal standards, and laws and rulings change.

OUR GUN-LOADED LANGUAGE

My baby shot me down! This is a phrase used to describe rejection, usually by a romantic interest. It is also a repetitive line in a song called "Shot Me Down!" recorded by Cher, and also by Nancy Sinatra, both in 1966.

9

A WORD TO WOMEN

"I WANT PROTECTION." SAID BELLA TO Zus Bielski in *Defiance* the 2009 movie, based on the true story of Jews hiding from the Nazis in the forests of Belarus. Everyone understands this need. We all have the need for protection; women, perhaps more so. Guns are often referred to as equalizers, meaning a skilled female, with a firearm, can defend herself quite nicely, thank you, against a larger, stronger assailant.

I actively encourage women to participate in gun ownership and training, as I do men. There is no reason why women should not enjoy shooting sports and hunting. Among the female shooters there are two exemplary American female Olympian marksmen (Should I have said markswomen?), Kimberly Susan Rhode and Amber English, both Olympic Gold Medalists in shooting sports. Rhode is an Olympic Double Trap and Skeet Shooter. Though her story is omitted by most media outlets, Kim Rhode has managed to shoot her way to six Olympic Medals, three of them gold, during the period from 1996 to 2018. She is a six-time national champion in Double Trap. She was the first Olympian to win a medal on five different continents! (Kim Rhode-Wikipedia en.m.wikipedia.org viewed on 22 May '21) More recently, Amber English snagged gold at the 2021 Summer Olympics in Japan for near-perfect scores in the Women's Skeet *competition. (Olivia Reiner, USA Today, online post, July 26, 2021)*

In her book, *Shoot like a Girl,* Mary Jennings Hegar, recipient of the Purple Heart and the Distinguished Flying Cross with Valor, reported the following words from an unnamed Air Force shooting instructor, words she said she remembered throughout her career: "Women are physiologically predisposed to being excellent marksmen. It's about their muscle tone, center of gravity, flexibility, heart rate, respiration, and, in my opinion, psychology… A lot of guys let their egos get the best of them… The chicks come in here and have fun. I try to teach my guys to shoot like a girl when I can. You know the Soviets were extremely successful at using women as snipers during World War II."

And were they ever! Alex Arbuckle has a report on *The female terrors of the Eastern Front. The deadly Soviet women snipers that terrorized the Nazis (mashable.com/feature/soviet-women-snipers, viewed 15FEB2022)* The Soviet Army accepted 2,000 women soldiers to serve as snipers as Germany invaded in June 1941. Among them was a Ukrainian-born college student, Lyudmila Pavlichenco, who became known as "Lady Death". According to Arbuckle's report, she had 309 confirmed kills in less than a year; thirty-six of those were enemy snipers. After she was wounded four times, she was sent on tour to rally support from Great Britain, Canada, and the US. In a speech in Chicago, she told the assembly, "Gentlemen, I am twenty-five years old and I have killed 309 Fascist occupants by now. Don't you think, gentlemen, that you have been hiding behind my back for too long?" Fortunately, after the invasion was put down, she was able to continue her studies and become a historian.

OUR GUN-LOADED LANGUAGE

Call the shots: this phrase originated in military exercises as leaders directed fire to chosen targets. To "call the shots" means to take charge and give commands.

A woman's choice of firearm(s) will depend on perceived wants, needs, and circumstances. If you want a handgun for home defense only, I recommend a full-sized pistol or revolver, with good capacity, that is a good fit for your hand size and strength. Most women don't have Yeti-size hands like men. If you plan to buy a semi-auto pistol, you must be able to operate the slide stop (slide release), release the mag using the thumb, and rack the slide efficiently. You need to be able to rack the slide readily in order to clear a jam efficiently. All of these can be an issue due to, most likely, a training issue, an improper fit ergonomically for your hand size, or a lack of strength.

If you need portable protection, I recommend something small enough to conceal, but it should be one that you can shoot and operate well. Remember, smaller weapons, designed for concealability, are not necessarily built for ergonomic comfort. A colorful weapon may look like a toy to a child. Children are attracted to toys, enough said.

When you come in to purchase your firearm, it is best that you avoid any appearance that you might be buying the firearm for someone else. Do your FFL dealer a favor and pay for your gun yourself, out of your account, not that of someone else. BATF observers may be suspicious if the person paying is different from the one whose background is checked for the purchase.

I recommend concealed carry over open carry for women, with the proper training and permits, of course. Generally, an attacker may believe that a female is an easier target. If the bad guy sees a gun openly carried by a female, it may be that the evil doer will assume the female is weak and attempt to take her gun. Bad guys find guns attractive and useful; don't let them know you have one unless you intend to use it.

Another reason that I like concealed carry for women, is that women conceal differently. No one is surprised to see a woman carry a purse with a sturdy shoulder strap. In the concealed carry world, ladies' modest-looking purses may be specially designed to conceal a handgun. Here is the big advantage. When you are traveling through a high-risk area, you can have your hand down inside the purse, gripping your weapon, inconspicuously. This is better because you have control of your gun and there is no delay in reaching for it. Translation: faster draw. For men who want this advantage, there are tactical bags with shoulder straps designed for concealed carry. Men may also want to revive the fashion statement of the satchel you saw in the movie *Indiana Jones*, for this purpose.

If You Are Pregnant

This is a time to be careful. If you are pregnant, I recommend that you stay away from the noise of gunfire. You can protect your own ears, but there is little that you can do to protect the ears of your unborn child. A baby in the uterus will have fully developed ears by twenty weeks gestation. By twenty-four weeks, the baby will respond to sound. Some say that you should only worry about the noise of gunfire in the third trimester. But my question is, what about the early development of fragile auditory nerves and tissues? Just because the baby does not respond to the sounds in the beginning weeks, does not rule out the possibility of harm. Very little is known about the effects of loud noise on a developing baby. "But," you may say, "A baby is submerged in the amniotic fluid of pregnancy and the fluid should muffle the sound." Doubtless, this provides some unmeasured variable degree of protection. Just as sound travels in the ocean, affecting sea life, it can travel through the fluid of pregnancy. Your unborn baby is bathed in muted sounds from the outside. I find no data to say what level of noise is acceptable.

The intensity of sound is measured in decibels (dB), a word intended to commemorate the work of Alexander Graham Bell, inventor of the audiometer and the telephone. Normal conversations occur at 60 to 65 dB. As sound intensifies to 85 dB, there is concern for hearing loss with prolonged exposure. Most gunfire generates greater than 140 dB! Depending on the caliber and ammunition used, the noise level can reach 175 dB or more. This is three times the normal sound range and well above the level thought to cause harm. (American Speech & Language Association, post reviewed on July 21, 2021) Also, the surroundings may intensify the sound. In an enclosed space, such as an indoor firing range, the sound may be amplified to an even greater level. We *do know* that the sound of a single excessively loud shot can cause permanent hearing loss. "But wait," you may say, "What level of sound, or noise, is delivered to an unborn baby?" The simple truth is that we may never know. Researchers would have difficulty measuring sound that close to an unborn baby, and such a study is unlikely to be approved for ethical reasons. This is simply a reminder to you to be mindful of the unborn. A CDC/NIOSH report, *Noise-Reproductive Health,* states the following:

- Increased noise levels can cause stress. This can cause changes in a pregnant woman's body that can affect her developing baby.
- Sound can travel through your body and reach your baby. Very loud noises may be able to damage your baby's hearing.
- Ear plugs or earmuffs can protect your hearing, but if you are pregnant, the only way to protect your baby's hearing is to stay away from loud noise as much as possible. Also, remember that hearing loss can result from a variety of causes.

10

PROTECTING OURSELVES

Protections from eye injury, hearing loss, lead exposure, and squib hazards will help to assure that your gun ownership is a benefit rather than a drag on your health.

Protect your eyes. When you fire a gun, your eyes are very close to the moving parts of your shooting iron. That area is subject to powder blowback, flying spent cartridges, small amounts of vaporized lead, and possibly scatter shot. There is also the potential for ricochet events that could damage your eyes. Shooters need protective glasses. Most of us wear ordinary safety glasses, the kind you find at a hardware store. There are some over-the-counter safety glasses that fit right over your prescription glasses. UV protective shatterproof lenses are a plus. The optimal eye protection for shooters, though a bit pricey, is prescription shooting glasses or prescription safety glasses. The yellow tinted ones are a good choice as they improve contrast.

Protect your ears. The noise of close gunfire will likely be the loudest sound that most folks will ever encounter. What are the implications? *How Does Loud Noise Cause Hearing Loss?* This paper from the Center for Disease Control, explains noise-related hearing loss. Loud noise harms the inner ear by bending and stressing the tiny hair cells in the cochlea. Hearing loss from loud sounds can be temporary or permanent. It may be gradual or sudden in onset. Hearing loss may continue to progress even after the exposure to the noise has stopped. According to the CDC, even a one-time exposure to an extremely loud sound can permanently destroy hearing.

Hearing loss is a deceptive disability. While a gunshot wound injury is obvious; acoustic trauma caused by gunshot is not so easily understood. There's no blood. Adding to the confusion, is the fact that hearing loss may be temporary on a few occasions. This may embolden some shooters to continue their usual practices, believing they can toughen their ears to tolerate loud sounds, all the while, failing to realize that damage is occurring. The CDC report says that a loss of 30 percent to 50 percent of the cochlea stereocilia (those highly sensitive tiny hairlike structures that communicate sound into the nerves and brain) can occur before the damage is detectable by audiometry. Once lost, these hair cells don't come back. Signs of auditory damage in progress as posted by University of Michigan Healthwise Staff are:

- You have difficulty talking or hearing others talk over the sound.
- The sound makes your ears hurt.
- Your ears are ringing after hearing the sound.
- Other sounds seem muffled after you leave an area of loud sound. (02DEC2020, HealthwiseStaff, WilliamH. Blahd Jr., MD, et.al www.uofmhealth.org/health-library/tf4173)

How loud is too loud? As measured in decibels (dB), again, normal conversation is 60-65 dB. Prolonged exposure to 85 dB or higher is thought to reduce hearing ability. Reports from various sources place the loudness of gunfire in the range of 140 dB and higher, even beyond measurable levels. These numbers reveal the very real risk of hearing loss from exposure to the sounds of gunfire. I have noticed it is common for law enforcers, the military, and even shooting instructors to have some degree of hearing loss.

It is worth noting that longer barrel guns are slightly less noisy than shorter barrel guns of the same gauge or caliber. Surprisingly, handguns are significantly louder than long guns, according to Dr. Krammer, Ph.D., of Ball State University in Indiana. (Dr.

Krammer, Ph.D., *Gunfire Noise Level Reference Chart,* (with comments), https://earinc.com/gunfire-noise-level-reference-chart, viewed 17FEB2022)

The choice of ammo may influence loudness as well. Ammo that travels slower than the speed of sound, known as "subsonic", slower than 1125 ft./sec. produces a lower dB level. Faster ammo that breaks the sound barrier "greatly increases noise". The quietest ammo is the .22 LR, which generates approximately 140 dB—though quieter, 140 dB remains in the destructive range. (www.gunsandammo.com/editorial/5-best-subsonic-loads-22lr/367863# viewed 17 FEB2022)

Earplugs and earmuffs can reduce the volume of sound delivered down the ear canal. These are rated by a Noise Reduction Rating (NRR) system or similar. These ratings can tell you the dB volume reduction according to laboratory tests. Actual noise reduction may vary among individual users. Noise reduction is greater with muffs, than with ear plugs. Before you invest in muffs, try them on with your shooting protection eyewear to make sure they work well together. The BEST hearing protection is *a combination of muffs over plugs*, which reportedly reduces noise by 65 percent, and should be sufficient. (*How do I use Noise Reduction Rating (NRR) values to determine the protection provided by a hearing protector?* www.ccohs.ca/oshanswers/prevention/ppee/ear_prot.html)

An audiologist can make custom ear plugs that are more comfortable and provide still better protection.

The Not-so-Silent Silencers

Another approach to racket reduction is the use of a silencer, aka a suppressor.

The words "silencer" and "suppressor" mean the same thing: a device placed on the muzzle of a firearm for the purpose of sound suppression. Though the BATF calls them "silencers", "suppressor" is a better word, these only reduce the sound. They do not eliminate it. These are sold in various sizes matched to the firearm of your choosing. They are great because not only do they help protect the shooter's ears, but the volume of sound delivered to others in the vicinity is reduced as well. Your horse and hunting dogs might appreciate your suppressor. They have stereocilia that need protection too! A suppressor may protect lots of ears and prevent frayed nerves as well!

Before you rush out to buy a suppressor you need to know this: a silencer, aka suppressor, is an "NFA item". Apparently, in 1934, Congress associated these devices with gangsters and mass murder, and thought it prudent to include silencers in the National Firearms Act. Currently, the hoops to jump through to get one are: proving that you are older than twenty-one, completing a Form 4, getting fingerprinted, submitting a photo, paying for a $200 stamp, waiting months for approval, and finally purchasing the device. If you qualify, you can get them online and in gun stores. "Possessing an unregistered silencer … is punishable by a fine of up to $10,000 and/or ten years in prison. (01JUN2012 SUMMARY OF FEDERAL FIREARMS LAWS Department of Justice)

This excessive regulation of suppressors has the effect of denying access to ownership. Get to know your congressional representatives and senators. You should ask them to change the law and remove silencers from the NFA list. Many more readily available for shooters could help prevent some hearing loss, and we could all save some money. Remember to explain that they don't really *silence* the gunfire; they *do* help to protect hearing by reducing the noise. While you're on it, order a copy of this book for your representative!

Protect from Lead

Most of us know that lead has been removed from paint, water pipes, and most gasoline. We understand that lead has historically caused problems for children's developmental IQs, allergies, and kidney function. Lead can be harmful to adults as well, causing kidney issues, tremors, brain function problems, high blood pressure, skin problems, and in women, loss of pregnancy and premature births. (23FEB2021, Executive Summary, National

Toxicology Program monograph on Health Effects of Low-Level Lead)

Lead is all around us all the time. Numerous lead compounds occur naturally in air, soil, and water. Lead is in our food, even our "healthy" vegetables. A paper from PubMed (PMID 1100370, 1975) by GT Haar states that we consume 300+/- mcg of lead daily. The EPA tells us lead is found in products we use regularly. Products containing lead include: batteries, solder wire, PVC, insulation around electrical wires, fishing weights, leaded crystal, glazed pottery, cosmetics, and ammunition.

In the face of inescapable lead exposure in the environment, those who re-load often or shoot in abundance, need to take extra precautions. Mike Jones, aka Garand Thumb, stresses mitigation of lead exposure for shooters. ("Garand thumb" is also an orthopedic diagnosis, aka M1 thumb) Among his many YouTube posts on shooting and firearms, is one called *Lead Poisoning from Shooting* (https://youttu.be qzfwT7hY44). This post is a quick rundown explaining the risk of exposure for shooters and measures for mitigation. From his post we learn:

- Most ammo contains lead, both in the primer and in the bullets.
- When a gun is fired, lead is vaporized into the air.
- Some firearms blow gasses containing lead compounds back toward the shooter; among them are the semi-automatics, piston drives, and those fitted with suppressors.
- Depending on wind direction, shooting outside may result in less lead exposure.
- A shooter's clothing and boots may carry a small amount of residual lead after a session at the range. It is good practice to wash those after a range day.
- People who fire 250 or more rounds per week, such as professionals in training, are at greater risk of elevated lead levels.

Mr. Jones, an avid shooter, has lots of ideas to mitigate exposure. When he shoots at an indoor range, he wears a solder respirator, presumably because he is a high-volume shooter. He recommends avoiding food, drinks, and smoking in the range area, as well as keeping fingers away from the mouth, nose, and eyes, because ingestion is the most common path for lead poisoning. Copper-coated FMJ rounds reduce lead splatter and ionization by 90 percent. Wear gloves when you pick up targets and brass casings. Wash everything—hands, face, forearms, and clothes; clear your nose, and wipe down your firearms and boots after a shooting session, especially if you are going home to a young child. De-leading wipes are available at Walmart, Walgreens, and some gun stores.

The Danger of Squib

Squib Happens. Knowing about squib is critical. A squib is rare but can be catastrophic. Even a seasoned professional having all the best training and all the best equipment, in the middle of a live firefight, can get the dreaded *squib*. If it happens, the next shot fired from the gun is a greater threat to the shooter than anything the enemy can deliver. You must stop with that gun *immediately!* (Luke McCoy, 22SEPT2016www.usacarry.com/how-to-detect-squib/) This helps make the point:

One day I was carrying my Glock 27 and did the range "draw and fire" in its carry state, "CLICK"… Now, I have put hundreds of rounds through that pistol before that "click" and after my shock cleared I tap racked the pistol and it has run many hundreds of rounds since then. Heck, I even reloaded the round it "clicked" on, which had a nice deep primer strike, and it fired fine. BUT, that could have been the "click" that killed me or my family. This was my Glock! It is not supposed to happen. It was also very good defensive ammo. It may not ever malfunction again but I can never get the incident out of my mind. (Topic Author,

Surferdaddy, Senior Member, 31Mar2021 *Re: Contact shot, blast damage?* CHL/LTC Instructor NRA basic pistol/home firearm safety instructor. P.2 Texas CHLforum.com)

Here you have an expert, shooting a quality handgun, using good ammo. Malfunctions and misfires such as these can happen to anyone.

I am aware of an occurrence where three squibs happened in succession in the same pistol, same barrel. A gentleman had a Bersa Thunder 380. He was shooting cheap aluminum cased ammo. Three consecutive firing failures happened. It was a miracle that a catastrophic explosion did not happen. This person was a new shooter who didn't understand the danger of squib events. A gunsmith subsequently found three bullets lodged in the barrel. These were cleared. The gun, in this case, seemed to have escaped damage, as did the owner, fortunately. This shooter was given a quick education that he won't forget on the danger of squibs.

What is it? *Squib* is a retained bullet or fragment in the barrel that fails its mission. Why is it so dangerous? It blocks the exit out the barrel. The next load fired goes against this obstruction, building massive pressure. It can happen with any conventional firearm. As a result of a squib, handguns have been known to blow apart; rifles have shattered including the stock. Severe injuries to shooters have occurred to include hand injuries, traumatic amputation of thumbs, and various forms of head, dental, and eye injuries. Again, the occurrence is so very rare, possibly only one out of a hundred thousand rounds fired, that the topic is often overlooked in basic firearm instruction.

How will you know a squib is present? Sometimes, but not always, it can be detected by a change in the sound of the gunfire. It will sound weaker, a little raspy, more like a clicking sound rather than the throaty "pshew" that you usually get. Listen for it. Check demos on YouTube to help you identify the changed sound. Also, a change in recoil, usually decreased, may be your only clue. Never work with a firearm that seems quirky.

Watch what happens at the target. There should be a new puncture after each shot, or evidence of the bullet landing down range. Listen to and watch the shots of others who are firing at the venue with you. Not everyone knows about squib.

Teach your children, your spouse, and your anti-gun friends about squib. Bring it up occasionally to remind your gun owner associates. If you think someone near you at the range has a failed discharge, possibly a squib, do not hesitate to call "CEASE FIRE NOW!" If it is a false alarm, there is no harm and you simply raised awareness. If, indeed, there is a blockage in someone's barrel, you are a hero. Your reputation will be exalted to Supreme Gun Guru of the Range for at least a day or so.

What to do about it? If you suspect a squib, *do not fire another round until the gun is checked!* For a minute keep the gun pointed down range to make sure the problem is not a delayed discharge due to slow ignition in the cartridge. After this, pause to gingerly unload your firearm. In the case of a pistol, you may need to remove the spring and barrel. Inspect the barrel from the breach looking for obstruction. A small flashlight and a gun-cleaning kit will be helpful. The presence of obstruction, full or partial, confirms the squib. Put a dowel or cleaning rod down the barrel and tap the bullet out. Inspect the barrel for damage. Hopefully, you will have kept the packaging the round was sold in. It would be helpful to the manufacturer, if you could report the incident, giving them the lot number and specifics of the event.

How Can Squib be Avoided?

Squib events have occurred more frequently in improperly reloaded ammo, or cheap ammo. If you reload your ammo, you must meticulously inspect everything constantly. Avoid reloading if you are in any way compromised by fatigue, alcohol, drugs, time constraints, or environmental distractions.

If you simply buy fresh ammo, get it from a reputable dealer/ supplier. Keep ammo away from moisture that results in corrosion. Inspect rounds carefully; any deformity of the casing can reduce the "burn" causing a failure. Keep gun barrels clean and free of debris. Clean and correctly lubricate firearms after all practice sessions. Heavily used guns should be replaced as they wear out. Indentations other than rifling inside a barrel can trip the bullet out of its desired spin and potentially cause a problem. All that said, still, there may be squib events, even in the best of circumstances. Your greatest lines of defense are awareness of the possibility, and your alertness to the problem.

11

SHOOTING PRACTICE

GUN OWNERS SHOULD PRACTICE FIRING THEIR persuaders regularly. For urban dwellers this will mean either a trip to an indoor range or perhaps a visit to a country cousin who lives out where practice shooting is allowed. Think of your trips to the shooting range the same way you think of going to your gym. You go to both places to maintain fitness and to guard your health. Maintaining your familiarity with your firearm and training to improve are important; your life could depend on it.

OUR GUN-LOADED LANGUAGE

A Straight Shooter: this phrase refers to someone who is honest and dependable, a no-nonsense type. The "straight shooter" will always tell you the truth.

If, for some reason, you know that you don't qualify to purchase a firearm, the same applies to shooting at a range. If you know there is a problem, don't bother going there. The staff has the right to refuse access. Be aware that law enforcers spend lots of time in practice at public ranges. There will be camera surveillance as well.

A range experience will go better if you plan an advance visit to scope things out. Be sure to study the "RULES OF THE RANGE" posted by the facility: they may vary from site to site. Get a general idea of how the range operates. Introduce yourself to the Range Safety Officer (RSO). Find out what credentials and gear will be needed. Ask about gun rental if you need that. Will special ammo be required? Is the firearm(s) you want to bring allowed? Check hours and days of operation. Is a membership required? If membership is beyond your budget, ask about training sessions that include live fire on the range. Lots of classes are available for beginners through advanced shooters that include range opportunities.

These bits of info will smooth the day of your practice session. Find a friend to share your outing. Shooting targets is more fun if you have a competitor! Pack a shooting bag with eye protection, ear protection to include ear plugs and muffs, de-leading wipes and disposable gloves. Put your firearm in a case or holster; it makes people uneasy to see a bare gun approaching.

Upon arrival for your shooting session, you need to be drug and alcohol free and not overly caffeinated. Your demeanor should be pleasantly alert and respectful. Any odor of alcohol, slurred speech, or abnormal pupil size will result in access denied. The same goes for signs of anger, aggression, or any hotheaded behaviors. I know the majority of you would never act out, but these things need to be said.

The facility may require that a current driver's license or government-issued picture ID with current address be left at the check-in area. You will probably be asked to sign a waiver and show a membership card, if required. Pay, and get your targets and booth assignment. The best most economical targets are the ones with one bullseye in the center, and four more in the corners.

Once you are in the shooting area, stay alert, remember to follow all the rules for gun safety, and follow the range rules. Don your ear and eye protection early. Someone in there may be shooting large and loud. Clip your target to the cable and press the control button to send it down-range to the set point you prefer. The shelf in front of you is referred to as "the bench". You can place your gun on it as you load. The area beyond the bench is "over the firing line" and "down range". Keep your gun pointed down-range; treat it as loaded at all times. You should not take food, drinks, or smoking or vaping materials in there. These things may be a distraction, and a vector for lead to get into your mouth.

Be observant and respectful of other shooters. Stay alert for RSO commands. They have to yell for obvious reasons. It does not mean they are angry. Avoid conversation beyond a brief greeting to other shooters, unless they are clearly taking a break. Keep your shots in your lane.

If you are working with a firearm that has a manual safety, I recommend that you reset the safety after every shot fired. This will help you to build the habit of releasing the safety each time you shoot. Practice until it becomes automatic. This will be a godsend if you ever need to shoot emergently.

If you encounter any problems or see anyone breaking the rules, notify the RSO. Expect the RSO to correct you as well, if you are not getting things right. It is okay to ask them for advice. If something dangerous is happening, you are allowed to yell, "CEASE FIRE!" Don't be afraid to do that.

The range is not a good place to practice drawing from a shoulder holster. The draw from a shoulder holster puts you and others at risk as you grasp, lift, and turn the firearm. RSOs hate shoulder holsters.

Feel free to take your targets with you when you finish. Make sure your gun is unloaded. Wipe down your gear and pack everything carefully. You should wash your hands, forearms, and face before leaving the range. Change clothes ASAP and wash the range clothes separately. De-leading wipes for your boots are a good idea.

Practice Outdoors at a Remote Location

Shooting targets outside can be fun and a great way to get together with friends. I have done this a couple of times and I have some thoughts about how to make it safe and enjoyable. In planning an outdoor shooting event many of the guidelines for indoor shooting will apply. There are a few additional things to consider. Is shooting permitted in the chosen area based on state and local law? Do you have permission to be on the property? Is it likely that hikers or others may be in the vicinity? Is there easy access to the property for an ambulance in a worst-case scenario? Is there an adequate cell signal in the area where the shooting will take place? Is there a landline nearby?

Is there any risk to livestock, horses, or pets? The replacement cost of a beef cow approaches $3,000; grass-fed is more. Shooting someone's dog carries an extremely high risk of retaliation. Plan on pepper spray designed for dogs.

Begin by choosing a location where you can shoot into an earth berm, with consideration for what might be beyond the down-range area such as houses, barns, parks, or businesses. Your earth berm should be at least twelve feet high, or you may use a steep hillside free of rock outcroppings. Be considerate of neighbors and their sleep patterns, especially those working odd shifts. Check with them if you are unsure of their sleep needs.

Prepare the range by measuring out a span twenty-five yards or more from the planned location of the targets to the firing line. The width should be a little wider than the width of the earthen berm that is the backdrop. Establish a firing line, not to be crossed unless the designated RSO gives the okay. Mark the area with brightly colored rope. Set up shooting lanes if you wish. It will be helpful to have two tables; one to use as a shooting bench, and one off to one side to use for loading. Loading should not take place behind the people on the firing line.

Target holders should be placed down range in advance. These can consist of plywood or cardboard attached to two stakes. Avoid metal stakes. Another option for mounting targets is stacked rail-road ties, if you have them, reinforced with an earthen berm rear-ward. Targets can be tacked, taped, or stapled to these holders. You will need a cooler with bottles of water, and a tarp or tent to provide shade or shelter as needed. Tell your guests to bring a folding chair and binoculars. Don't forget a first-aid kit with two tourniquets. Bring a fire extinguisher. Need sunscreen? Bug spray? I almost forgot—targets!

You should appoint yourself or someone else to the role of Range Safety Officer (RSO). You should only invite people who are dependable, cautious types who take instruction well. I have noticed, in an informal setting like this, even seasoned militarily trained individuals tend to relax a bit too much and get a little sloppy with etiquette and safety. From the outset, you must establish that the Four Rules of Safe Handling *will be followed,* and: there will be absolutely NO alcohol or drugs. There will be NO goofing off, and NO practical jokes involving firearms during the outing. NO firing without the RSO's go-ahead, and NO firing up into the air. I recommend that you post written rules of safe handling and go over them before anyone starts.

The RSO should communicate clearly the order of activities and who may shoot when. Nobody shoots until the RSO gives the signal. Changing the targets, also, requires the RSO's supervision. For this process, all guns must be emptied and down on the bench with all hands off. The RSO must give permission before anyone enters the target area.

You may choose to make the event(s) a competition… or not. It might be fun to compare abilities using different types of firearms. Or, you might appoint someone to judge to see who has the best accuracy. Shooting from a prone position off the bed of a truck might prove interesting. It's all up to the imagination. If you give prizes, be sure to include one for "most improved" and "best sport".

12

THE REGULATION OF FIREARMS

What Are the Regs?

FIRST, HERE IS A SHORT TEST to check your knowledge of restrictions on your use of firearms. Answers are at the end of this chapter.

1) The best thing to do if I feel threatened is to fire a warning shot into the air. True or False?
2) The best way to deal with my neighbor's kid flying a pesky drone over my property is to shoot it down. True or False?
3) In my state, you can open carry, with no permit, so it is okay to go into my local Post Office armed. True or False?
4) Those twenty-one-gun salutes at military funerals are fine. True or False?
5) More people die in mass shootings each year than from any other gun-related cause. True or False?
6) I can legally carry my firearm across state lines. True or False?
7) What if I have a firearm in my car and there is a law enforcement traffic stop?
8) I can ship my rifle to my cousin in Kissimmee. True or False?
9) I can take my weapon on a plane. True or False?
10) It must be okay to take my gun into a National Park; the wildlife can be aggressive. True or False?

11) Anyone can buy a firearm online. True or False?
12) I can buy a gun to donate for the church raffle. True or False?
13) My sister can buy a firearm as a birthday gift for her husband. True or False?
14) It is okay to take my ten-year-old to the range. True or False?
15) Rubber bullets are pretty much harmless. True or False?
16) Should I buy a concealed-carry handgun because I am dealing with an aggressive dog in my neighborhood when I go out for a walk?

Answers will be provided at the end of this chapter.

OUR GUN-LOADED LANGUAGE

Don't Shoot the Messenger: this is a reminder not to direct hostility toward the innocent bearer of unwelcome news. Alternatively, "When the messenger arrives and says, 'Don't shoot the messenger,' it's a good idea to be prepared to shoot the messenger, just in case". —Howard Tayler, cartoonist

Regulation of Firearm Ownership

The first step in understanding the regulation of this $63.5 B per year firearms industry, is to look back to the Second Amendment in the Bill of Rights of the Constitution of the United States of America, an entitlement so many politicians and media types would prefer to forget. It states, "A well-regulated Militia, being necessary to the security of a free State, the right of the people to keep and bear arms shall not be infringed." In 2008, the Supreme Court reaffirmed the Second Amendment right of *individuals* to "keep and bear arms" for self-defense and other lawful purposes. According to this ruling, individual gun owners retain the right to gun ownership, with no requirement that they belong to a militia.

Robert F. Kennedy, Jr., in an appearance on Fox Nation and interviewed by Tucker Carlson, stated that due to the many restrictions imposed during the Covid pandemic, with exception of the right to bear arms, all our rights promised in the Bill of Rights were discarded in the span of only one year. He said of the Second Amendment, "It's the only one that's left. We have to love our freedom more than we fear…" (Kennedy, R., Jr. interview Fox Nation, Tucker Carlson Today, viewed 16NOV2021)

After the Constitution, the next order of regulation is with the US Congress. In 1934, in reaction to Chicago's Valentine's Day Massacre, Congress enacted the National Firearms Act (NFA). The NFA enabled the Federal Government to tax and regulate the shorter-length long guns and unusual concealable guns. You can see quite a collection of these "unusual concealables" on display in the International Spy Museum in DC. They may bear little resemblance to a firearm, but look remarkably similar to a cane, an umbrella, a camera, a cigar or other paraphernalia.

Another provision of the 1934 NFA was a plan for federal *registration* of certain guns. This provision was effectively taken down by the Supreme Court in 1968. That same year, Congress enacted the Gun Control Act (GCA). This act was not intended to inconvenience law-abiding gun owners. Yet, it contains a sweeping array of restrictions and federal regulations. It requires federal licenses (FFL or Federal Firearms License) for any business entities engaged in the various aspects of the firearms industry, including the production and distribution of ammunition. It includes the mandate that dealers maintain sales records. The GCA prohibits direct mail order sales, blocks most interstate sales of handguns, and gives the US Attorney General authority over specified imports. An example of this is that President Biden's administration was able to block ammunition manufactured in Russia from coming into American markets. Also, the 1968 GCA imposed the first federal restrictions on who may purchase a firearm. (viewed online 9/27/2221gunpolicy.org/firearms/citation/quotes/6678).

A very surprising decision from the Supreme Court in June 2019, may have upended a section of GCA code, and opened the door for illegal, undocumented immigrants to possess firearms and/or ammunition. The Court ruled that such a person possessing a gun and/or ammo may be *innocent* unless *the court can prove* two points: 1) that the individual had full knowledge of his illegal immigration status and 2) that the individual had the knowledge that *possessing a firearm* in that status is illegal! (France, O. 21June2019jurist.org/news/2019/06/is-supreme-court-rules-in-favor-of -illegal-immigrant-in-possession-of-firearm/) I can understand how the guy may have failed to understand that his student visa had been revoked. What puzzles me is his attorney's argument that a lack of understanding that his use of a firearm was forbidden was seen by the court as a reasonable defense. In my world, "ignorance of the law" has never been a defense, but I am no judge! I defer to the Supremes! For sure, this muddies the water for those of us in sales. How am I supposed to know what an illegal, undocumented immigrant knows about our laws or about his/her legal status! Do I sell them ammo, or no? Even more weird, as I understand the report, the less the immigrant understands, the more accommodating the system will be toward their ownership of firearms and ammo. See me, shaking my head!

OUR GUN-LOADED LANGUAGE

Bring out the Big Guns: a person or thing of improved power and influence.

Another important federal law is the Brady Handgun Violence Prevention Act of 1993. Those who are old enough, will remember March 30, 1981, the date of the assassination attempt against President Reagan. Six .22s were fired from a Rohm RG-14 revolver by a would-be assassin named Hinckley. Four people were injured, including the President. James Brady, the White House Press Secretary and the most severely injured, sustained skull shattering head trauma. He lived thirty-three more years. Though he was severely disabled, with help from his wife, he lobbied for reforms that resulted in the Brady Law. (reviewed9/28/21en.m.wikipedia.

org.wiki/James_Brady) The Brady Law, an amendment to the 1968 Gun Control Act (GCA), added a five-day waiting period, and a *background check* before transfer of ownership of a handgun to an unlicensed individual (buyer). Currently, the background check requirement still stands and applies to all firearms. (viewed 9/28/2021atf.gov/rules-and-regulations/brady-law)

Enforcement of the Brady Act of 1993, falls into the purview of the (federal) Bureau of Alcohol, Tobacco, Firearms and Explosives. You know them as the "BATFE", aka, ATF. Even before Brady, the ATF was busy. Among ATF's activities were: investigation of arson, dealing with threats to homeland security, tracking illegal drug runners, backing local police when needed, credentialing federal firearms licensees (FFLs), education and prevention of infractions of federal law, and overseeing the precepts of the GCA.

With Brady, came a requirement for background checks on all potential civilian gun buyers and many others involved in armed public service. The enormity of this undertaking led to the creation of the digitized National Instant Criminal Background Check System (NICS) through a coordinated effort of the FBI, ATF, DOJ, and state and local law enforcement agencies. The "Instant" checks eliminated the need for the five-day waiting period. In 2019, the most recent year posted, the NICS system processed 28,369,750 background checks. (2019 NICS Operations Report, fbi.gov) The volume has grown since then. This federal screening program denies the possession of firearms to the following categories:

- History of conviction of a crime punishable by more than a year in prison
- Fugitive from justice
- Unlawful use or addiction to controlled substances
- Identified as mentally defective or committed to a mental institution
- Illegally or unlawfully in the US
- Holding dishonorable discharge from US Armed Forces
- Former citizen who renounced US Citizenship

- Subject of restraint order due to harassing, stalking, or threatening an intimate partner or partner's child
- Any conviction of domestic violence
- Under indictment for a crime punishable by imprisonment for a term exceeding one year

NICS checks are initiated by the gun buying applicant's completion of an ATF 4473 form. (fbi.gov/services/cjis/nics/about-nics) It is important to be truthful when completing the form. Convictions have resulted from fraudulent information on the application.

Keep in mind that a background check is NOT a gun registry.

Currently, there is no formal federal gun owner registry in the US, though some states may have them. A national registry is a hot-button issue for gun owners, which they have successfully fought off for almost ninety years. Findings of an individual's NICS check will simply report, "PROCEED", "DELAYED", or "DENIED". This information is kept confidential and disclosed only to the applicant, or to the FBI/ATF when legally ordered.

However, the firearm sellers, the FFLs, are required to maintain logs of all firearm sales for twenty years. If a seller goes out of business, these records are turned over to the ATF. A report from *Law Enforcement Today* asserts that under the Biden administration, the ATF has begun to assemble a database on gun buyers using the logs surrendered at the closing of FFL businesses. If true, this would create an off-the-record federal gun registry. The report goes on to explain that the establishment of such a database is illegal under current law. (McKinley, M. 'Did Biden's ATF just acknowledge they already have a federal gun registry and are keeping data on gun owners.12Nov2021www.lawenforcementtoday.com/did-bidens-atf-just-acknowledge-they-have-a-federal-gun-registry/)

One other point regarding the NICS program is that not all states participate in the NICS program. Some states have their own, more stringent systems for background checks.

The preceding has highlighted some of the prominent federal firearms regulations and institutions. Bear in mind that state and local governments usually write codes for firearms as well. There are thousands of firearms regulations. It will be important to the individual gun owner to keep abreast of federal, state, and local ordinances. Yes, it is a lot of information! Some sources recommend that you contact your State Attorney General with gun law questions; others say consult a lawyer. A source known as *handgunlaw.us/* is recommended on the Wilson Combat Channel of YouTube by Massad Ayoob, a well-known firearms instructor. With disclaimers, this site attempts to track the many varied and ever-changing local firearm regulations.

Adding another wrinkle to the legal scene is *Printz v. United States*. Once again, the Supreme Court delivered a zinger! You will recall that the Brady Act of 1993 was an amendment to the Gun Control Act of 1968. Brady required background checks before a gun is transferred to new ownership, as happens when a gun is purchased. The language of the amendment required the Chief Law Enforcement Officer (CLEO aka sheriff) of a buyer's area of residence to examine IDs and applications associated with any firearm purchase. Local sheriffs were tasked with digging up background information on any buyers from their districts. It bubbled up that Sheriff Jay Printz, aka CLEO, of Ravalli County, Montana; and Sheriff Richard Mack, aka CLEO, of Graham County, Arizona, had more important things to do than to examine documents all day, especially since they had never signed on to work for "the fed". These were the two who took it to court, though there were many other sheriffs who empathized with their position. By December 3, 1997, their case had made its way to the Supreme Court. The Supremes waited until June 27 of the following year, but they *overturned* the lower court decision and freed the two sheriffs of this odious responsibility. This is fascinating, in that it left sheriffs free to "voluntarily comply with the federal mandate", or perhaps not. (en.wikipedia.org/wiki/Printz_v._United_States) The implication is that sheriffs are free to determine what *federal* regulations they will enforce! If this decision had gone differently, we probably would not have the NICS program in place now, and most likely you would be waiting five days to purchase a firearm! This decision was hailed as a major victory for states rights, or federalism, as well as a triumph for locally elected sheriffs.

On a good day, the NICS application process runs efficiently, and background checks are accomplished within minutes. However, there have been episodes when reports were delayed. If the NICS report is delayed out beyond three days, the seller is free to continue the sale without it. Such was the case when Dylann Roof purchased a handgun in West Columbia, SC, in the spring of 2015. You may recall that he's the guy who fired on and killed nine people in the historic Emmanuel African Methodist Episcopal Church of Charleston, SC, in June that year. The fact that he was able to purchase a firearm due to this system glitch became known as the "Charleston Loophole".

Apparently, the "Loophole" was still open during the gun-buying surge of 2020. Reportedly, a huge number of firearm sales went through without background checks during that summer because the NICS system was simply overwhelmed and unable to deliver within the three-day window. The headline for *Health – September 16, 2020,* reads, "Almost 300,000 guns sold without background checks as pandemic overwhelmed system." But FFL gun stores are able to use their own discretionary policy when waiting on any NICS check status of proceed, delay or denial. Also every business in the US has the right refuse service to anyone. (https://bigthink.com/health/guns-pandemic/)

As you approach the purchase of a firearm, you can smooth the process by having your identifying documents up to date. If you have moved recently, especially into another state, be sure to update your license or ID with the current address. Never falsify a government document. There are parties who would make an example of you, your sales person, and the FFL that is the source of your purchases.

Now, about the test at the beginning of this chapter; how well did you do?

Test Answers and Discussion

1) The best thing to do when I feel threatened is to fire a warning shot into the air. False. Ethan Siegel, Ph.D, Astrophysicist, and number-cruncher, writing for *Forbes*, recommends that guns never be fired up into the atmosphere. Gravity will win, and the bullet will return to Earth at a speed that can easily penetrate a human body. Remember two and two. The bullet can stay aloft up to two minutes and return to Earth as far as two miles away. Dr. Siegel's article lists six victims of such gunfire, three of whom were children who died. (Siegel, E., Jul 2,*2020forbes.com/sites/startswith-abang/2020/07/02/the-science-of-why-firing-your-gun-up-into-the-air-can-be-lethal/?sh=c27b8f4ff656)*

2) The best way to deal with my neighbor's kid flying a pesky drone over my property is to shoot it down. False. *The Federal Aviation Administration (FAA) classifies drones as aircraft, and shooting down an aircraft is a felony.* (Moise,T,5/11/2018wfmynews2.com/article/news/drones-what-are-my-rights/83-551453733)

3) In my state, you can open carry, with no permit, so it is okay to go into my local Post Office armed. False. *"No person on U.S. Postal Service property may carry or store firearms… punishable by fine, and/or imprisonment up to a year!"* (Poster 158, October 2019aboutusps.com/posters/pos158.pdf) U.S. LawShield, a legal defense firm, carries this further, stating that having a gun in a car in the Post Office parking lot is a violation. The regulation is 39 C.F.R.232.1(1). (2016Dec.2016uslawshield.com/post-office-parking-lots-it-wont-be-a-merry-christmas-if-you-are-in-jail)

4) Those twenty-one-gun salutes at military funerals are fine. True, *because they use blanks.* (Siegel,2020)

5) More people die in mass shootings each year than from any other gun-related cause. False.

Americans tend to think that gun-related deaths are primarily from murders and mass shootings. In fact, suicide by gunshot represents 60 percent of all gunshot deaths. (APM Gun Survey, Part Two: Causes of gun-related deaths. a pmresearchlab.org. viewed 13NOV2021) The number is approximately 20,000 yearly, while mass shootings, sad though they are, only result in counts in the hundreds. (Bump, Philip, 2021 has already been a very bad year for mass shootings July 7, 2021 washingtonpost.com)

6) I can legally carry my firearm across state lines. True for some states. If you are traveling, there are apps to help you know which states allow open carry and/or concealed carry.

7) What if I have a firearm in my car and there is a law enforcement traffic stop? It is impossible to over-emphasize the importance of how you handle this situation. I will explain this in detail, because traffic stops have resulted in tragedies to officers, as well as to those being pulled over. Remember, the officer may not know anything about you. Keep your registration and driver's license readily available. At the first blink of a blue light signifying that you are being pulled over, you should slow down and find a place on the right side of the road wide enough for the officer(s) to greet you from either side of your vehicle without being exposed to the flow of traffic. Take your time, go slow, and use your flashers to let the officer know you are cooperating. If you are in doubt that the traffic stop is legitimate, you can call 911. You have the right to find a well-lit place where you feel safe. Pull over, stop, set your park brake, and turn on your interior light if it is dark outside. Lower the front windows, right and left, enough to allow communication. Turn off any entertainment devices. Turn off the ignition. Anticipate that there may be a second officer who will approach your vehicle on the right side. This officer may not know about any instructions given by the first officer. It will be important that the second officer sees that you are not a threat. Place both hands on the steering wheel and keep them there. You can retrieve the license and registration later when prompted. The officer needs to be able to see your hands and the hands of your passengers. (How to Talk to Police,criminaldefenselawyer.com, viewed 08Oct2021) Keep your hands high on the steering wheel and have your back-seat passengers place their hands on the backrest in front of them. The person on the passenger side, front, should keep hands visible on the lap. (Stradling,R , 18 APR2018,do you know what to do when a police officer pulls you over? NC has new guidelines. amp.newsobserver.com/news/traffic/article193751114)   Expect to wait a few minutes while the officer reports your tag numbers and communicates with dispatch. Everyone should remain inside the vehicle and stay buckled. When the officer approaches, he or she will introduce himself/herself and explain the reason for the stop. (North Carolina Division of Motor Vehicles, North Carolina Driver Handbook, Ch.4,p.47) If there is/are firearm(s) in the vehicle, you must tell the officer this in the least threatening way possible, and the location. If you have a concealed carry permit, and you have a firearm on your person, you must tell the officer of this as well. Have your valid Driver License, Registration, and Concealed Carry Permit ready to hand to the officer. Then say "I have my Concealed Carry on me how can I help?" Your best bet is to stay calm, polite, cooperative, and as understanding as possible. Make no sudden moves. Avoid digging or reaching for anything.

Avoid arguing. This is no time to make your case. You will have that opportunity in court. If you sign the citation, it is not an admission of guilt.

A tragedy happened in Minnesota, in 2016, that illustrates the importance of clear communication and adherence to instructions during a traffic stop. The heart wrenching video from the girlfriend of the victim, Philando Castile, is still available on the web. I urge you to find it and draw your own conclusions. It all started with a broken lens on a tail-light. The officer involved was ultimately acquitted at the trial, and I am not trying to second guess the decision. From reviewing the case, and seeing her video and hearing her comments, it seems to me that failed communication contributed to this tragic loss of Mr. Castile's life. He had communicated to the officer that he was licensed to carry and that he had a firearm, as was expected. It appears that he was told to keep his hands on the steering wheel, which he did, until he was asked to provide his driver's license. That reaching movement toward his hip pocket, was interpreted by the officer as a move to draw his weapon, and the officer opened fire. Castile was shot five times and died about twenty minutes later. (Killing of Philando Castile,en.m.wikipedia. org, viewed08OCT2021)

How do you explain five shots at close range?

Why would a law enforcement officer engage in multiple rapid-fire shots after the suspect has already been wounded? The answer may be found in another report, from a terrible, awful day with the FBI. Law enforcers draw from a body of science and case reports that guide police practice in real time. A report from a deadly Miami shootout April 11, 1986, may explain the thinking of law enforcement even now, more than thirty years later.

On this occasion, FBI agents were engaged in a firefight with two armored-car robbers. One FBI agent was able to land a shot into the chest of one of the robbers. Though the round missed the suspect's heart, this was, according to a subsequent forensic report, a lethal injury. Despite having sustained a solid torso hit, the suspect was able to return fire. He killed two FBI agents and severely wounded two more. This carnage was possible, because, even after a lethal chest injury, the suspect was able to return fire for several seconds to minutes. (Miami Shooting 4-11-86, FBI Records: The Vault vault.fbi.gov, viewed 13NOV2021) This is an illustration of how Hollywood is often wrong about the lethality of a single gunshot.

Mike Callahan, writing for Police 1, states that even when the suspect's "heart is destroyed", the injured party may continue for ten to fifteen seconds, a very long time in a firefight. (Callahan, Mike, Why bullet size matters in officer-involved shootings, www. Police1.com-ammunition, viewed 12NOV2021) For this reason, officers are instructed to fire rapidly and continue until the threat is "neutralized". I was surprised to see this acted out and later explained to a junior investigator in the movie series, *The Terminal List,* with Chris Pratt.

These case reports underscore the need for perfect compliance with law enforcement, at traffic stops and on any other occasion of the interaction between law enforcement and the public. However, in the Philando Castille catastrophe in Minnesota, it appears that the driver *was* compliant with the traffic stop.

Yet, as he reached for his wallet to retrieve needed documents, the perception of the law enforcer was that gunplay was imminent. My suggestion to prevent such a misconception in the future, is that we borrow an idea from the advanced life support teams. First responders understand the importance of clear communication. They do it this way: if, during a resuscitation exercise, an order is given by a code leader, the responding team member repeats the phrase back to the leader. As an example, the leader might call for a "shock now". The responding team member holding the defibrillator, repeats back, "Shocking now—all clear!" before administering the shock. Restating the order confirms to the leader that the order is understood and being carried out. Restating also serves as a safety break allowing time for a course correction if the order has been misunderstood. I think this concept could have applied to Mr. Castile's unfortunate traffic stop. If, before responding to the request for his driver's license and moving his hands from the steering wheel, he had said, "I will move my left hand from the steering wheel to my left hip pocket for the driver's license", and paused for the officer's approval, there might have been a different outcome. Hopefully, such an event will never happen again.

8) I can ship my rifle to my cousin in Kissimmee. True, you can, but you have to ship it, UN-loaded, of course, by USPS or by common carrier to a federally licensed retailer, FFL, in your cousin's area (Handguns only go by common carrier). You will need to declare the contents of the package as a firearm. Your cousin will have to submit to a NICS background check, before he/she can take possession at the FFL site. (nssf.org/articles/giving-a-firearm-as-a-gift—some-reminders-from-nssf, viewed 10/1/21)

9) I can take my weapon on an airplane? True, but not in your carry-on, and not on your person! Commercial airlines can accommodate firearms, firearm parts, and ammo as long as TSA requirements are met. Contact the TSA and/or the airline for instructions and follow them carefully to avoid civil or criminal penalties. Firearms, parts, or ammo may NOT be in carry-on baggage.   (nraila.org/articles/20150101/guide-to-the-interstate-transportation) Add destination state policy and copy of airline policy inside the box.

10) It must be okay to take my gun into a National Park; the wildlife there can be aggressive. Answer: Maybe. It varies. The National Park Service allows firearms in the parks BUT state laws take precedence. Gun owners are to contact the state and local authorities for guidance. (nps.gov/articles/firearms-in-national-parks.htm) Be alert for temporary restrictions as well; these may be related to criminal investigations. The website listed above is a great source to consult if you will be visiting a National Park.

11) Anyone can buy a firearm online. False. Online buyers are subject to the same background requirements and identity checks as in-store customers. To purchase a firearm online, you should begin by contacting a retailer near you that is an FFL, and one that is willing to work with you to run the background check and be responsible for the transfer. Advise them of your intentions, and then make your online purchase, providing the needed contact information and shipping address for the FFL where you would like to pick up the item. (Cleckner, R., Mar20,2020, How to Buy a Gun Online, gununiversity.com) When you are notified that your purchase has arrived, in order to take possession, you will need to present an ID with your current physical address to the FFL. You will have to complete ATF form 4473 for a NICS screening, if that is the system used in your state. Only a few states manage background checks differently. The NICS report should be ready in a matter of minutes. Remember the FFL hosting this transfer makes no money on the purchase, so you should expect to pay a fee for their services. As soon as your background check is approved, The FFL will collect the processing fee and transfer the firearm to you.

As with any online purchase, be aware there may be fraudulent online dealers, so be cautious.

12) I can buy a gun to donate for the church raffle. False and no. What can be perceived as a Straw Purchase. When one is buying a firearm for someone else and receiving some kind of compensation.

13) My sister can buy a firearm as a birthday gift for her husband. True, she can, but it might be more hassle than she anticipates. Laws vary by state and locale, and she needs to be sure her husband qualifies for gun ownership. Several states require the transfer of ownership to be conducted through a retail FFL, which defeats the excitement of opening a gift box with a big shotgun. The ATF strongly recommends simply giving a gift card instead of making the purchase outright. (nssf.org/articles/giving-a-firearm-as-agift-some-reminders-from-nssf/)

14) It is okay to take my ten-year-old to the range. True. Most shooting ranges allow minors in with a parent. Contact the range in advance to get their policies regarding minors.

15) Rubber bullets are harmless. False. Rubber bullets can inflict significant injuries and death. Lacerations, facial disfigurement, and serious blunt trauma have all resulted from "less-lethal rounds, aka, rubber bullets". (Ng,Mforbes.com/sites/mattng/2020/07/10/this-is-what-rubber-bullets-and-less-lethal-rounds-can-do-to-you/?sh=2ceb4a835a4d) These "less lethal" bullets were used during the Israeli-Arab conflict, in 2000, resulting in blunt and penetrating trauma injuries to the face, chest, back, and abdomen of those involved. (Mahajna, et.al. 'Blunt and penetrating injuries caused by rubber bullets during the Israeli-Arab conflict in October, 2000: a retrospective study. *The Lancet* (British Edition), 2002-05-25,Vol.359(9320),p.1795-1800.)

16) Should I buy a handgun for dealing with an aggressive dog in my neighborhood when I go out for a walk?

Answer: Carrying a firearm with intent to shoot someone's dog will create more problems than you are anticipating. Don't use a gun where pepper spray or a high-pitched whistle will do. I think carrying a handgun is fine, but take pepper spray for the aggressive dog.

Hostile Active Shooter Scenario

Are you and/or the injured party(s) in further danger, as in an active shooter situation? In this case, rounds from your own weapon returning fire may be the best medicine. Eliminating the threat will help you and others avoid becoming additional victims. Ask any combat veteran.

If you are unarmed, defenseless, and facing an active shooter, most self-defense courses will advise you to run away fast if you have a reasonable exit. If leaving the scene is not an option, conventional advice is simply to hide quietly. This script means that you will abandon the injured and save yourself. No heroics are recommended.

Alternative behaviors to consider

What you do in the event of an active shooter is highly individualized. Only you know your strengths and weaknesses in that terrifying moment. Despite the law enforcers' response in the Uvalde school shooting, current thinking is that individuals who have mentally rehearsed a shooter scenario, will be better able to think and act effectively in an active shooter crisis. Reviews of the mass shootings of the last decade have shown a woeful lack of preparation of the public to deal with mass/active shooters. Though we will never have prospective trials to help us understand the correct course of action as bullets fly, we can study these events in retrospect.

If you happen to be among an unprepared group coming under attack, the best reaction is to put distance and barriers between the shooter and potential victims. Run! Run in irregular zig-zags and curves to keep the shooter off target.

Unfortunately, criminals often know the environment and movements of their prey. A perpetrator may choose a site where there is no means of escape. When potential victims are confined, they generally duck, crouch, and take cover; or they may look for a way to fight, despite the shooter's advantage.

Consider this lesson from nature: I have noticed that when a yellow-jacket's nest is disturbed they scramble! Some decide to sacrifice themselves and attack despite being outsized and out gunned by the threat. Others move out; emphasis on *move*! Their tiny brains seem to know that a moving target is less likely to be hit; their chance of surviving is greater if they keep moving! I have to think this is a lesson for people caught in a hail of gunfire. The crouch and cower response is ill-advised in my opinion. A deranged shooter is emboldened by victims when they become easy stationary targets; yet, this is what we teach. We should learn from the yellow-jackets and teach a scrambling response.

OUR GUN-LOADED LANGUAGE

A very old proverb says: forewarned is forearmed. Another way of saying this is that advanced information empowers.

13

STORIES THAT FOREWARN

Tales of Three Texas Tragedies

THE FIRST TRAGEDY HAPPENED NOVEMBER 5, 2017, at the Sutherland Springs Baptist Church. In this attack on unarmed congregants, twenty-seven people were killed by a lone gunman. Among them were several children, a pregnant woman, and her unborn child. The ages of the victims ranged from pre-born to seventy-seven years old. There was no resistance to the attack from inside the church and the gunman strolled freely up and down the aisle shooting the defenseless. Resistance only came as the shooter left the church and was engaged by an armed Sutherland Springs resident from across the street. The assailant managed to drive away from the scene. Later, he was found dead in his vehicle, out near the county line.

Fast forward to December 29, 2019, to the West Freeway Church, also in Texas, where another gunman opened fire on a congregation during worship. On this occasion the gunman was only able to shoot two people due to the swift action of a dedicated security team. Shortly after the earlier attack in Sutherland Springs, the West Freeway Church, being forewarned, had organized a volunteer security team under the tutelage of Jack Wilson, a licensed firearm instructor and Federal Firearm Licensee. Though many guns were drawn inside the church that day, the volunteers showed remarkable control and restraint. Mr. Wilson fired the single shot that neutralized the threat in this situation.

He received the Governor's Medal of Courage. "I don't feel like I'm a hero. I feel like I did what I needed to do to stop an evil threat." He credited preparation, training, and a willingness to act as the overriding factors that contributed to fewer lost lives, when his church came under attack that day. Comparison of these two cases demonstrates the value of preparation.

A third ordeal in a Texas place of worship, known as Congregation Beth Israel, on January 15, 2022, provides another example of the importance of training to survive. Unlike the events at Sutherland Springs Baptist Church and the West Freeway Church, where the assailant opened fire early, the gun wielding terrorist in the Synagogue held the Rabbi and three others as hostages for eleven long hours. The Active Shooter Training of the congregants from the Secure Community Network, provided by local police and FBI, is credited for the safe escape of all four hostages.

The backstory is that the Rabbi remained calm and comforted the others, as the terrorist gradually became more agitated. Rabbi Cytron was able to maneuver himself and the others into a position near the exit. At a moment when the gunman laid his weapon down to pour a soda, the Rabbi yelled "Run!" as he lobbed a chair at the gunman. It worked out great. All the hostages escaped as the FBI SWAT team from Quantico moved in. Things ended with the hostage taker downed by unspecified gunfire. (17JAN2022 nypost. com and 18JAN2022 cbsnews.com/news/Texas-synagogue-hostage-malik-faisal-akram-suspected-gunman-details)

Comparisons of outcomes among these three attacks on houses of worship, clearly demonstrate the benefits of advance preparation and training. These lessons can be generalized to other venues where people gather. A survivor of the Synagogue ordeal, Jeffrey Cohen, posted, "We weren't released or freed. We escaped because we had training from the Secure Community Network on what to do in the event of an active shooter. This training saved our lives—I am not speaking in hyperbole here—it saved our lives." (Fallert, Nicole, 18JAN2022 www.buzzfeednews.com/amphtml/nicolefallert/texas-synagogue-hostage-rabbis)

Another Case for Preparation to Save Lives

An active shooter scenario can bring on an active bleeding scenario, as was reenacted in the movie, *5:17 to Paris.*

I highly recommend this thought-provoking flick, which is based on a true story of the August 21, 2015 terrorist attack on a Thalys train enroute from Amsterdam to Paris. The leading actors were real-life participants during the actual attack. The three brave Americans who put down the attacker, rendered first aid, and calmed fellow travelers, are Spencer Stone, Alek Scarlatos, and Anthony Sadler.

The movie takes you onto the train as Stone and the others respond to an active shooter and administer aid to a passenger who suffered a severe neck injury. The viewer is given a sense of the moment, as passengers come under fire. You will see some very realistic scenes depicting the management of a severe wound to the neck and shoulder area.

Scrolling back to Stone's Air Force training, a great line comes off as he was required to explain his unorthodox responses during an active shooter drill at a training facility. In response to the irate captain who mocked Stone for the fact that he had armed himself with a ball-point pen, while taking a position by the door to the classroom, his reply was, "I just didn't want my family to think I died hiding under a desk!"

Spencer Stone's bravery on the train proved not just to his family, but to the world, that he would not be found hiding under a desk! The three, along with a British citizen, Chris Norman, were awarded the French Legion of Honor, by then-President Hollande of France, and, later, they received awards from President Obama.

Seeing this true story reenacted will help to prepare you to deal with a gunshot wound/blood loss event. I urge everyone, even non-gun owners, to think how he or she might respond to an active or potential shooter. It is better to have a plan so there will be some prospect of stopping the carnage. Begging mercy is not an option, it only emboldens the attacker.

Your response time will be improved if you have previously reviewed scenarios and developed a routine of heightened awareness of surroundings.

14

WOUNDED

What will you do if someone is shot? What if that someone is you? If an injury occurs, your ability to think and react may be critical. For this reason, any gun owner should think ahead and prepare for the unexpected. This would include keeping a first aid kit with bandages, a tourniquet, sterile water or saline water, and gloves. Your preparation should also include a course in basic CPR, basic resuscitation, refreshed every other year. A basic CPR course is offered by the American Heart Association and by the American Red Cross and others.

The First Minute After the Blast.

The first order of business after the blast, is to quickly assess the situation. This initial survey will determine the best early actions. Just as military operators are taught to have a heightened sense of awareness of their surroundings, so too should civilian gun owners constantly assess the threats and assets around them. The source of a gunshot may not be easily identified. The source may be the victim, accidental or intentional. You will need to make a quick determination of your personal safety before you give aid.

Is the Injury a Suicide Attempt?

You probably know of someone who committed suicide using a gun. I say this because, in all-cause gun death data, suicide is far more prominent. Suicide by gunshot occurs more frequently than gun murders, mass shootings, and firearm accidents. A whopping 60 percent of gunshot deaths are suicides. Most people don't know this, and the lack of understanding impedes prevention efforts. (Druzin, Heath, *The Majority of U.S. Gun Deaths Are Suicides, But a New Poll Suggests Few Americans Know It*. Gunsandamerica.org/story/19//10/01the-majority-of-gunshot-deaths-are-suicides-but-a-new-poll-suggests-few-americans-know-it/)

Suicide attempts by gunfire are extremely lethal. The survival rate is low and very different from other gunshot injuries, whether intended or accidental, where there is approximately a 70 percent survival rate when all injury sites are included. For this reason, once the gun is fired, in an act of suicide, especially to the head, rescue efforts may be futile. This naturally puts the emphasis on PREVENTION! Approximately two-thirds of all gunshot deaths in the US are suicides, not police actions as popular culture would have you believe. This amounts to 23,000 suicide deaths by gunfire annually. Among them are about 1,200 children and teens.

These tragic suicide numbers are rightly viewed as a public health issue. However, for perspective, note that untimely deaths from drug overdoses far exceed all deaths by gunshot injury. Overdose deaths have recently risen over 100,000 per year.

A suicide attempt using a firearm is the most lethal method generally available. These attempts by gunfire result in a 90 percent death rate as opposed to only about a 10 percent death rate from other methods chosen for suicide. (Firearm Suicide in the United States, everytownresearch.org, last update 1.8.21) Sadly, males tend to direct their weapons to the head, and even if they survive they are frequently blind and otherwise disabled. (*Survivors of Self Inflicted Gunshot Wounds to the Head* Characterization of Ocular Injuries and Health Care Costs, JAMA Opthalmol.Author Manuscript in PMC 2016 December 21)

My fellow gun owners, we can do better! It is imperative that we clean this up. All gun owners should develop an awareness of suicide of all kinds and the symptoms. Look for sadness, moodiness, hopelessness, sleep problems, sudden calmness, withdrawal, changes in personality and appearance, self-harm, recent trauma or life crisis, threatening suicide or talking about suicide. (www.

webmd.com, Mar 11, 2020) If these behaviors/events are noted in those around you, access to firearms should be blocked by secure firearm storage, which should be routine anyway.

Oddly, another symptom may be the lifting of depression and a surge in energy. It is thought that an improvement in mood comes from the fact that the individual has prepared a plan for suicide. They may see it as a plan for escape.

If the person exhibiting symptoms is YOU, there is no loss of dignity in asking a trusted friend or family member to keep your firearms until the crisis is over. Remember, easy access to guns is probably the greatest risk factor. Firearm owners should review the topic of suicide prevention frequently. Some sources of instruction are: American Foundation for Suicide Prevention and Mayo Clinic, *Suicide and Suicidal Thoughts (http://www.mayoclinic.org/disease4s-conditions/suicide/basics/symptoms/con20033954   ).* The National Suicide Prevention Hotline number is 800-273-8255.

Know the Source of Gunfire

Will you put yourself in danger if you give aid? Is the injured party down? Is he/she breathing? Conscious? Confused? Bleeding? Just a little or a lot? Control of rapid bleeding takes priority over other resuscitative efforts. What body part is penetrated? What was the ammo? Did the blast cause other injuries such a fracture from a fall? What is the environment and proximity to medical care? Where is your phone? Who can help? Has anyone called for help? What lines of support are available? Do you have a tourniquet and first aid materials available? How long will it take for help to arrive? What should you do while you wait? Just know that it would only be natural to be nervous and even a bit panicked as you deal with a fresh injury. It's okay and normal. In this chapter, I will walk with you through some thoughts and plans for early intervention for injury. The following is not a substitute for formal safety and life support instruction.

Gunshot wounds can occur literally anywhere, at any time, and to anyone. As a gun owner, you should go through life support and first aid training with special attention to emergency trauma management. Locally taught and on-line courses are available through the American Red Cross and the American Heart Association and others. Careful with the on-line courses; the internet is rife with frauds.

Accidental gunshot injuries are largely survivable. These injuries usually result from a lack of safety training, inattention, a lack of knowledge, a lack of safety habits, and poor etiquette. The degree of damage from a gunshot wound (GSW) will depend on the range of the shot, the caliber of the bullet, and the body parts injured.

The following is a brief sketch of injuries by body locus and what you might expect. Again, this is not a substitute for basic training in first aid and resuscitation. I am presenting this overview to further interest in first aid for gunshot injuries.

Head wounds

These are the most lethal because the brain may be compressed by swelling or by an unwanted accumulation of blood inside the skull. The resulting build up in pressure cannot easily be relieved because the cranium is essentially a closed space. If pressure on the brain is increasing you may see agitation followed by drowsiness, followed by unconsciousness. However, the injury may be severe enough to shear away part of the skull, in which the bleeding and brain may be exposed, with a resulting decrease in pressure on the brain. Call for help ASAP! While you wait you can check pulses and pupils. These maneuvers are explained in basic life-support classes, which I highly encourage. Keep the patient warm while you wait. If there is no evidence of neck injury, the brain-injured patient may fare better in a position with the upper body and head in a slightly raised position, if you can safely make that happen.

In the event that the shot has caused a glancing head wound, know this: a person's scalp is loaded with tiny veins and arteries, vessels that bleed easily. Loss of copious amounts of blood from the scalp does not necessarily mean there is a severe injury. This type of head injury is readily survivable. You can put a cloth or bandage on it and apply gentle pressure to reduce the bleeding while you wait for help.

Neck injury

The anatomy of the neck is complicated. It connects the brain, and airways to the rest of you. The brain needs blood to flow in and out and that depends on some important blood vessels passing through the neck. Another critical structure in the neck is the wind-pipe (trachea) that puts air into the lungs and brings it out again. Spinal cord injury will be covered separately. Management of a wound here is tricky to say the least. If the victim is bleeding, you cannot use a tourniquet! You will need expert care ASAP! Call for help immediately. Talk to the victim. Encourage the victim to stay awake. Just as you see in *5:17 to Paris,* you may need to put a makeshift bandage and gentle pressure on the wound. If you see an artery pumping in squirts with each heartbeat, it's ominous. You should try to control that with your fingers clamping tight onto the ruptured blood vessel until help arrives. Try not to worry too much about clamping a pumper. The blood was being lost anyway and the Good Lord graciously provided more than one artery to supply the brain. And, in a stroke of genius, He put in a circle system inside the walnut to supply blood where needed despite an artery being closed off. Try not to be overwhelmed by excessive blood loss. People can survive surprising amounts of blood loss. However, a big arterial bleed can be fatal in as little as two minutes. While you are there, check for breathing. Sometimes an unconscious person's tongue can fall back and block the airway and stop their breathing. A good way to control this in an emergency, even while you clench onto the bleeding artery, is to pull the jaw forward. This has the effect of moving the tongue out of the air space of the throat.

Chest wounds

The most likely injury from accidental gunfire is a chest wound and I encourage gun owners to be familiar with first aid for the same. Since the lungs occupy the largest area within the chest cavity, a bullet to the chest is likely to injure the lungs. Other important structures such as the heart, great blood vessels, and esophagus may be injured as well. An entrance wound to the chest may be so small as to be overlooked, especially if the victim has other injuries. Some bullets traverse the chest cavity and leave an exit wound that is often larger than the entrance wound. Be alert for exit wounds. If you are the first on the scene of a gunshot injury, your priority, after calling for help, should be to control any *rapid* blood loss to the outside of the body wherever it is occurring by using tourniquets or compresses.

In thinking about a chest wound, consider the vital functions of the heart and lungs in keeping oxygen-rich blood at enough pressure and volume to adequately supply the brain. Consider also that the heart and the lungs work similarly in that their function is to repeatedly fill and empty out blood from the heart and spent air from the lungs. Everything works by precision changes in pressures and volumes within the chest. The entrance of a bullet disrupts the mechanics of these functions. Where there was negative pressure for breathing air into the lungs, there may now be a positive pressure from the outside air entering through the bullet tract onto the "wrong side" of the lung. This unusable air can become trapped inside the chest and cause one or both lungs to collapse. If there is a noisy air sound at the site of a chest wound, it will likely be a "sucking chest wound". This can be treated by placing an occlusive material, like a clear plastic wrap over the entry wound. If, however, the victim's breathing becomes worse, it likely means that the unwanted air is crossing from the inside of the damaged lung with each inhaled breath. You should then remove the occlusive dressing to relieve any pressure working against the lung expansion.

Similarly, any bleeding that develops around the heart may cause an unwanted pressure against the outside of the heart and decrease the volume of blood available for the heart to pump. These problems require advanced emergency management. Until help arrives, reassure the victim and keep the person warm and awake if possible. If there is a loss of consciousness and a loss of pulse, follow basic life support guidelines. Continue to talk to the victim and reassure him or her even if the person seems unresponsive. Hearing is the last of the senses to go when someone becomes unconscious.

Spinal Cord Injury

Spinal injury is a dreaded event that conjures up images of life in a wheelchair or machine dependence for breathing. Modern science has been able to create gain-of-function viruses, but we have yet to find the magic to restore a severed spinal cord. That said, there is progress and hope for those suffering spinal injuries.

Gunshot wounds can cause spinal injury directly to the spinal cord, or indirectly by a variety of means. Cord injuries can result from bone fragmentation on impact, which creates additional projectiles inside the body, or the injury can come from abnormal twisting, over-stressing neck positions. Cord compression, which is sometimes treatable, can come from pressure on the cord due to blood or fluid buildup around the spinal cord. Spinal cord injuries can be the result of headbanging falls as well.

Regardless of the entry point of the round, first aid providers should be aware of the possibility of spinal cord injury. I hope everyone is paying careful attention to the next two statements because they are important. *Those first on the scene should be aware that moving an injured person can cause a spinal injury where none existed before and an improper move can extend a partial spinal tear injury.* Spinal cord damage can be permanent . Bone fragments are usually sharp. The spinal cord is surrounded by a stack of interlocking bones called vertebrae. These bones can fracture with or without damaging the indispensable spinal cord. We simply cannot see, when we are out in the field of fire, where fragments may have lodged. Unless the injured party is in a place of imminent danger, he or she should only be moved by those who are trained, and who have the equipment to do the move safely. (Mistovich, J., Med, NRP & Karren. K. PHd,EMT-B with Werman, H. MD, *Prehospital Emergency Care,* 11th Ed. Pearson Pub. 2018)

If the care of this fresh injury falls to you, as in all emergencies, call for help immediately. As you avoid moving the injured person, you should try to keep him or her from moving the neck or back. If there is profuse bleeding or choking or other imminent danger you may have to move the person. Do so as carefully as you can with help from others when possible. Avoid letting the casualty's head roll in any direction. Try to keep the head and neck in line with the lower back. Avoid flexing or twisting any part of the neck or back. Stabilize the head and neck however you can, with whatever you have, even if it is only field stones. While you wait for help, gather as much information as possible about the event. Watch your injured party carefully for bleeding, loss of pulse, problems breathing, pain, drowsiness, or unconsciousness. Never give up on someone with severe injuries; until our awesome medical teams have had the opportunity to apply their expertise, and believers have prayed for healing.

Abdominal wounds

The victim of a gunshot wound to the abdomen will likely have penetration of the intestines in addition to damage to other organs, blood vessels, and nerves. After paying attention to the basics of calling for help, checking for rapid bleeding, pulse, and breathing, the first responder should attend to the wound. Expect a report of severe pain and nausea. The most comfortable position will be supine (lying on his/her back) with hips and knees slightly bent to relieve any pulling pressure on the wound. The injured party may assume this position on his own. If you need to move the person, think of possible spinal injury in addition to the abdominal wound. If the abdominal wall is lacerated, the intestines may spill out and become exposed to the air and to contamination. Keep everything as clean as possible; infection is a huge risk long-term. You may notice an odor if the large bowel has been torn. Any twisting or drying of the gut should be avoided. In the less-than-optimal field conditions, a sprinkling of lukewarm water may be preferable to letting a section of bowel dry out. A cover of plastic wrap will help keep moisture in. A light bandage dressing is a good idea, if you have it available. It will keep the injured person from seeing the extruding abdominal contents. Looking at one's own severe injuries can cause shock. In addition to watching the breathing and checking pulses, the caregiver should look for a possible exit wound. Evidence of excessive bleeding, internal or external, include: pallor or ashen color of the person's skin and lips, rapid breathing, and a weak or absent pulse at the wrist. Even on a warm day, an injured person can develop hypothermia. Try to keep the sufferer warm and calm while you wait for help.

Injury to an Arm or Leg, Hand, or Foot

Injuries to arms, legs, hands, or feet frequently result from faulty firearm discipline, with the injured party being shot by his/her own firearm. The type of bullet or shell will impact the extent of injury. Parts involved can be skin, soft tissue, muscle, nerves, blood vessels, and bone. As with the other firearm injuries, the first responder should begin by assessing the threat of further injury to self, others, or the one already wounded. If all are in a relatively safe place, the first responder should have someone call for help, simultaneously moving to control any rapid, especially pumping, bleeding.

Think tourniquet. In the event of a gunshot wound, attention to rapid bleeding takes priority. With a severe injury to large arteries, an adult can bleed out and die in five minutes or less. A tourniquet may be lifesaving with this injury. You should keep tourniquet(s) in your first aid kit. They won't take up much space and are lightweight. You may apply more than one tourniquet if the injured person is bleeding from two or more extremities.

I encourage all readers to enroll in basic life support classes (BLS), with the understanding that application of a tourniquet is not usually taught there. It will be up to you to learn this skill and *be ready to apply it!* Please don't wait until someone is bleeding to dig around in the back of your truck and try to remember where the tourniquet is stashed. A pool of red goo pumping out is a panic attack. This is no time to Google instructions. You need to rehearse with your tourniquet because your ability to think and function may be impaired in the first moments after an injury happens. Consider that unopened packaging may be an impediment to your response time. The tourniquet I own came tightly wrapped and vacuum sealed in heavy plastic. It was difficult to open. Once it was open, there were extra distracting items in the package: gloves, gauze, dressing materials, and instructions. This underscores the need for you to open and identify these items before you need them. You should familiarize yourself with your gear, read your instructions, and do a practice run occasionally in advance. Later, your bleeding buddy will appreciate it.

For bleeding of an extremity that is amenable to a tourniquet, it should be applied two inches above the wound, and tightened until bleeding stops. If you are unable to tell where to place the tourniquet due to clothing, blood, and/or distorted anatomy of the limb, it will be okay to apply the tourniquet high on the extremity, as close to the trunk as possible. You may have to apply the tourniquet over clothing. The race is to get the bleeding slowed, preferably stopped. If the tourniquet fails to stop the bleeding, you can add a second tourniquet above the first. No tourniquet available? Improvise. Use what you have. A belt, a rope, a ratchet strap, Bungee cord, or similar item may serve the purpose of getting heavy blood loss under control.

Some sources advise loosening the tourniquet at intervals to allow blood to flow to the limb. I recommend against that; if help is on the way, you should wait and let the experts manage the release of the tourniquet.

If with your initial assessment, you find only trickle bleeding, it can wait a bit while you perform an assessment of pulse, breathing, alertness, and/or other injuries. Begin basic resuscitation if needed. If the injury appears to be simply a wound to the extremity and the person is awake, you may then turn attention to the wound. You may find the limb positioned at some strange angle, which would tell you the bone is likely shattered. You should gently bring the injured part into a normal position, using a gentle traction to prevent the bone fragments from grinding. Be aware that bone fragments can further the damage to nerves, muscles, and blood vessels when the arm or leg is moved. A supporting splint may help prevent further damage. You can use a board, a couple of layers of cardboard or possibly, a rolled blanket to help stabilize the extremity. Apply the cleanest dressing you have and reinforce it if there is continued bleeding.

The foregoing has been a brief sketch of first-aid interventions for gunshot wounds. This review is intended only to raise awareness and encourage further education in first aid.

OUR GUN-LOADED LANGUAGE

Bite the Bullet – A coping mechanism for enduring pain in the absence of anesthetics, dating back to the 1700s. The phrase is used figuratively to mean prepare for pain related to the upcoming necessary action.

Retained Fragments and Bullets, A Hazard for Survivors of Gunshot Injuries

This section should be of interest to health-care providers. The existence of an old gunshot wound should be recognized when a candidate presents for subsequent unrelated medical care. The possibility of retained bullets, shot, or fragments should be considered as part of patient assessment. While the patient may be reluctant to volunteer this data, health-care providers should be aware that after a gunshot wound, lead shot and/or bullet fragments can be retained for years after an injury and ignored. There exists a significant number of cases in which retained lead fragments are recognized but surgical removal has been deemed too risky to attempt. This information is important for two reasons: 1) Some retained metals can move and cause internal injury if the patient is subjected to MRI scanning. A lodged bullet may have a bi-metal jacket which is attracted by a magnetic field. 2) Retained lead can possibly lead to chronic lead poisoning, and even death.

"Clinical symptoms are the mainstay for the diagnosis of lead poisoning. Unexplained abdominal pain, motor neuropathy in the extremities, sensory neuropathy, poly-arthralgia, and neurological disorders are the most common symptoms. *Burton's line*, a dark line between the teeth and gums, is one of the clinical signs of lead poisoning." (*Lead poisoning induced by gunshot injury with retained bullet fragments.*J-S Yen, T-H Yen 20MAY2021QJM:An International Journal of MedicineVol.114,Issue12, published online) Also, anemia, kidney damage, spontaneous abortion, and behavioral changes have been reported. This wide assortment of findings could easily lead to diagnoses unrelated to lead poisoning. This underscores the need for careful history taking.

Lead levels can be determined from blood samples. If lead toxicity is diagnosed, and surgical removal of the lead particles is not an option, the condition can be treated by use of an oral agent. This chelator binds with the lead and facilitates excretion of the lead from the body.

15

PREEMPTING UNPLANNED DISCHARGES

Prevention/Gun Safety/Unplanned Gunfire

CLEARLY, PREVENTION IS PREFERABLE TO MOPPING up after a firearm injury. Safety is always a bargain compared to the alternatives. Safe gun handling and storage is underrated until it's too late. Almost all unintended firearm discharges could be prevented if handlers followed the safety rules, repeated here for you.

Four Rules of Firearm Safety

[1]
Treat all firearms as if they are loaded.

[2]
Always keep your firearm pointed in a safe direction.

[3]
Keep your finger OFF the trigger until ready to fire
and target is in sites.

[4]
Be sure of your target, what lies around it, and beyond it.

Safety failures can come from improper maintenance, improper storage, improper handling, or improper access by people who are not able to think rationally, or by children. Lethal and disabling injuries can happen as result of so-called "accidents" with firearms. Some folks explain that *any* unintended discharge from a firearm is preventable and unacceptable, saying there is no such thing as an "accidental" firing; there are only negligent unplanned discharges. Unwavering safety disciplines and etiquette are key to lowering the already inflated statistics that threaten more infringement.

I want to give you more information about unintended firearm discharges, but my research comes up short. My search for information on the subject "accidental gunshots" yielded surprisingly little. I have talked to other people who are aware of many unplanned firearm discharges, yet, my media search yielded no substantial reviews, no opinion essays, and no case reports. Perhaps episodes of unplanned discharges are underreported because the subject is an embarrassing, sometimes painful, topic.

I wanted to know which specific activities involving guns were more likely to result in unplanned discharges. Is cleaning a gun a high-risk event? What about climbing over or under fences while carrying a rifle? Moving in and out of vehicles? I felt that this type of information could be helpful to gun owners, and others.

My Informal Survey of Unintended Firearm Discharges.

In response to the information shortage, I pulled together a brief, informal survey, a pilot study of sorts to see if any specific activities stood out. The reports are from random adults who volunteered the information and who will remain anonymous. They were free to describe any unplanned gunfire event for which they had knowledge. There was no time frame and no requirement to divulge any identities. Some responders reported more than one occurrence. Not all requested information was available on every event studied.

The Survey:

Accidental Gunshot Survey

Do you know of a time when a gun went off unexpectedly?
Date__________, Type firearm_________________ Approximate year
of the event___________.
Check: Nobody hurt____, No property damage_____ Yes, property
damage______, Injury,____, Death____.

Please circle Yes, or No.

Were children involved? Yes or No
Was the gun being cleaned at the time? Yes or No
Was the user crossing a fence? Yes or No
Climbing into bed? Yes or No
Clearing the gun of ammo? Yes or No
Holstering or unholstering? Yes or No
Goofing off? Yes or No
Dropping the firearm? Yes or No
Was the accidental discharge due to drug or alcohol consumption?
Yes or No
Other: ____
How did this happen? ____
How could it have been avoided?_______________________________

My Findings

I was able to collect reports on forty-one incidents. These findings have not been verified; this survey is informal. The responders have no reason to give any false reports that I can determine. There would have been more reports in the count, but my social media censored the content, and Google Surveys would not allow my survey onto their platform, even for pay. Why a gun safety survey is inadmissible was not explained.

Of the forty-one responses, "goofing off", or playful behavior with a firearm, was checked twenty-nine times, *outranking all other categories combined!* This could imply that abandoning safety and etiquette in gun handling is *the most serious problem* to address regarding unplanned firearm discharge. For this reason, I am adding this fifth rule to the Rules for Firearm Safety:

FIVE Rules of Firearm Safety

[1]
Treat all firearms as if they are loaded.

[2]
Always keep your firearm pointed in a safe direction.

[3]
Keep your finger OFF the trigger until ready to fire
and target is in sites.

[4]
Be sure of your target, what lies around it, and beyond it.

[5]
No GOOFING OFF with a firearm. No play acting.
No gun tricks. No practical jokes – NEVER!

The next highest category, "incidents involving children", or minors, had six occurrences. Outcomes for the children were three deaths—two of them teenagers and one a four-year-old. The person who reported the first teenager's death explained, "He thought the safety was on." The second teen death happened due to a gun discharging when a younger child followed an older pre-teen, crawling under a wire fence. The younger child's air rifle discharged hitting the older one on the back of his head, causing heavy bleeding and possibly a seizure. The four-year-old's death occurred when he found a loaded handgun among the sofa cushions. As reported in local news, his parents were smoking marijuana and playing cards in the next room.

There were two non-lethal injuries to minors. One injury was a BB to the neck that penetrated the skin. The other was a BB into the eye, resulting in permanent loss of vision. (Yes, just like the oft-repeated warning in *A Christmas Story*.) Two or more children acting together were noted in four of those six cases. This would suggest that children playing together are at greater risk.

The third highest category was "Drug or Alcohol Involvement" with three definite entries and two other possible ones—10 percent of the total. Of these, there were three occurrences of property damage including damage to interior walls and to exterior concrete.

Two gunshots happened as guns were being cleaned. One resulted in an injury to the hand, the other, in the destruction of a person's kneecap. I found only one incident for each of the following: crossing under a fence, climbing into bed, clearing the gun of ammo, and "holstering/unholstering". Unholstering a handgun, resulted in an injury to the arm of a bystander. Removing a long gun from a rack in a pick-up truck resulted in a self-inflicted injury and the death of a young man who was a husband and father.

Pulling all these findings into one short summary is a bit jarring, even though this is a small study. This is an accumulation of reports from dozens of people over their lifetimes. I did not control the time of the occurrences. Some happened a couple of decades back, while many of the events are relatively recent. Remember, too, that we only asked for reports of mishaps, with no regard for countless hours of safe gun management.

I was impressed by the diversity of those inadvertently setting off their firearms. There were seasoned military types, including a Marine, a soldier in training, and a Navy veteran. Also in the mix was a farmer, an attorney, a customer in a gun store, a hiker, a hunter, and others right down to the age of four. The big shock in this report was the number of children involved and the lethality in that younger group. Of all forty-one occurrences studied, three resulted in the deaths of minors. That's just over 7 percent of this entire study group.

There were two reported deaths of adults to add to the three children's deaths, five total. Three of the five lethal, unintended discharges were self-inflicted. The four-year-old, reportedly, was alone when he found the handgun and shot himself. All of those who lost their lives were middle-aged or younger, much too young to die. These events cry out for mindfulness in handling and storing firearms. No firearm should ever be within the reach of a toddler. Even so, toddlers can be taught to recognize a gun and associate it with danger. Little ones should be taught to run away and find a trusted adult if they find a gun. After the toddler stage, children should be taught respect for firearms, basic firearm safety, and they should be taught that they can NEVER play around with a gun. Firearms should be locked safely away from children and any other incompetent person.

There were no findings of female involvement with firearm mishaps in my study. This is likely to change; women are moving to gun-ownership in greater proportions than ever before. As of this writing, a female who has resigned as a police officer after twenty-six years, is in court defending herself for what she says was a panic-driven mistake. In the widely publicized case of the death of Daunte Wright, Officer Kim Potter admitted she drew and fired her Glock handgun thinking it was her taser. This case proves unplanned discharges can happen to anyone. Her case will likely be studied in police academies, and possibly lead to changes in police training and in protocol for carrying their emergency gear.

I wish to thank those who volunteered information for this informal pilot study. The findings are food for thought. As always, further and more formal study is needed.

YouTube has a helpful video produced by Paul Harrell, entitled *Most Common Types of Negligent Discharge*. Mr. Harrell's statements match mine, in that needed data on unintended gun blasts is not readily available. In contrast to the findings from my informal study, his impression is that improper training and poor gun handling techniques are the main problem.

He highlights scenarios that lead to surprise discharges. He identifies the following problems: 1) failure to engage the safety 2) failure to keep the trigger finger *off the trigger until ready to fire* 3) failure to appreciate or understand chambering of a round in a magazine-loaded gun 4) going back and forth on the mechanics of a double-action revolver, resulting in empty chambers rotating with loaded chambers 5) accidental loss of thumb control of a revolver hammer 6) unloading mistakes. 7) wrong holster 8) wrong holster strap placement. This is a neat video that I heartily recommend. He does a great job of explaining these problems as well as the fix for them.

IN SUMMARY

THE PREPARATION OF THIS BOOK HAS taken on added significance as the process coincided with a bleak time in our history, the second year of the great Covid Pandemic. Using the pandemic as grounds, government officials tossed Constitutional rights and assumed "emergency powers" to govern by mandates. Gun owners cringed as freedoms guaranteed by the Constitution seemed to evaporate in the face of Covid hysteria. Schools and churches were closed. Many small businesses were closed as governing officials determined which ones were deemed "essential" and allowed to survive. Daily death and hospitalization counts dominated the news, terrifying the general population.

In the fall of 2021, Robert F. Kennedy, Jr., of the Children's Health Defense and counsel to a personal injury practice, released a book which is an overview of public health issues. Shortly afterward, he gave a pivotal interview that focused primarily on our failed management of the pandemic, and on his concerns for governmental overreach. In summarizing, at the forty-minute mark he methodically delineated the loss of freedoms guaranteed by the Bill of Rights. He stated, "During that year we literally got rid of every amendment to the Constitution except the Second Amendment—the only one that's left." (Kennedy, Jr. Robert F. *Coup de Vax* Tucker Carlson Today Fox Nation 15NOV2021)

THAT got my attention. He had entered my wheelhouse. I am passionate about the Second Amendment, the right of free citizens to bear arms. I, like almost all gun owners, have no desire to inflict pain and suffering on another human being or even an animal. I will, however, staunchly support the Second Amendment, which is the right to self-defense, or in another sense, the right to avoid becoming a victim.

Closely overlapping the Covid pandemic, the world has sadly witnessed the Russian invasion of Ukraine. "After decades of strict gun control laws, the Ukrainian Parliament changed its tune … voting to decriminalize gun ownership for self defense." – Aidan Johnston, March 2022. (www.thewashingtonexaminer.com)

The reversal went like this (2022):

Feb. 22 – The ban was lifted that prevented most civilian ownership of firearms.

Feb. 24 – The government of Ukraine was passing out AR-15s "like candy" as civilians lined up to receive them. More than 10 thousand were distributed.

Feb. 26 – A spokesman reported that Ukraine has more fighters than guns, as he begged for more from the West, especially sniper rifles. Mike Tobin reported lines for gun distribution streaming out around the corner beyond view at one of the police headquarters.

Feb. 27 – A seventy-nine-year-old grandmother was interviewed as she was shown taking up arms. Her message essentially was, "They may kill me, but perhaps I can help save the life of a younger person." A young mother stated, "If I were not holding a baby, I would take the gun, for there is no other way of stopping this!"

There were calls for more ammo.

Feb. 28 – "I don't need a ride; I need more ammunition!" – President Volodymyr Zelenskyy of Ukraine.

Mar. 04 – Ammo, Inc. of Wisconsin donated 1 million rounds to load AK-47s in Ukraine.

Mar. 04 – Commentator and Veteran Joe Joey Jones remarked on the fact that "untrained civilians" were taking up arms to defend their country.

(The timeline above was taken from various news reports during the early days of the Russian Invasion of Ukraine.)

Would Ukraine have fared better early on if they had had a well-armed, well-trained citizenry? Are small arms a deterrent to violence? Could a fight like this ever happen on American soil? Could our defenses and infrastructures be interrupted? These are questions for free people to decide for themselves. Certainly, our founders established the freedoms needed to defend ourselves.

My book is now a part of a greater conversation, and it is significant for its fresh approach to examining the freedom of firearm ownership. I have built into the narrative topics not usually found in other gun-related media. It is not enough just to be good with a gun, it is also important to understand the significance of guns in our history, our culture, and our ever-threatened freedoms. The more we know and understand, the better we will be at managing this asset for good. It is my hope that others will find courage to write about these and similar topics, putting firearm ownership in its proper place. If all goes as planned, my readers will come away knowing that if we are to retain this Last Right and restore all the others, we must rise to meet the challenges aligned against the Second Amendment.

Mr. Kennedy said that our rights are a gift to us, purchased through the sacrifices of the people of 1776. Our Declaration of Independence says that our rights are endowed by the Creator. Pray we can keep them.

GLOSSARY
YOU GOTTA SPEAK THE LANGUAGE

air gun – Handguns and/or long guns that use compressed gas for propellant. These include BB guns, pellet guns, and air rifles.

AR 15 – An ArmaLite 15, a firearm that resembles the original design of Marine Eugene Stoner. The AR-15 is one of the most popular firearms sold currently in the USA and in other countries.

action – *n.* The mechanism of a firearm that acts upon the cartridge or shell to deliver gunfire. The parts of a firearm that work together to load, unload, fire, and eject the cartridge. Some types of action are, revolver, bolt-action, break action. lever-action, pump, and semi-automatic.

arms – *n.* Weapons, firearms.

armorer – *n.* A person responsible for arms and ammo to a working unit, as in a military unit, or a sporting event, or an entertainment event such as a movie set. The origin of the word pre-dates the era of firearms when knights needed suits of armor for jousting.

armor piercing – *adj. phrase* Describes dense bullets that can penetrate hardened targets. These may be made of hardened steel, tungsten, copper, or hard alloys. Depleted uranium has been used as well. (www.explainthatstuff.com/bullets.html#cartridge, viewed 15OCT21)

assault weapon – *n.* This term is lacking a clear definition. It is usually found in literature that supports more governmental gun control. It is frequently intended to describe firearms that mimic military weaponry.

ballistics – *n.* The science of projectiles and firearms. (The Reader's Digest Oxford *Complete Word Finder* 1996)

BATFE – *n.* Bureau of Alcohol, Tobacco and Firearms and Explosives, a law enforcement agency that operates under the United States Department of Justice.

bean bags – *n.* refers to a "less lethal" shotgun ammo that contains #9 shot and sometimes colored chalk in a Kevlar sock. These should not be fired into anyone's head, neck, or spinal area unless the intent is to injure the individual.

boattail – *n.* Describes a bullet shape that tapers to the rear, giving better flight characteristics and a longer range.

bolt action – A type of rifle mechanism that is charged by manually pulling back, then forward, on a curved bolt charging handle to eject a spent casing and load the next round.

break action – A firearm design having a hinge that allows the "break" to expose the breech for loading. Example: Smith & Wesson Model 3 Scofield revolver and/or a side-by-side over and under shotgun.

bullet – The projectile shot from a rifle or pistol.

bullet proof – Resistant to penetration by bullets.

bullpup – *n. or adj.* A firearm design in which the action is positioned behind the trigger mechanism. Bullpups are easier to handle and the barrel length is equal to a longer rifle, preserving accuracy.

bull's eye – Center of a target, often used as an exclamation to mean perfect placement of a shot. Also, "dead on".

bump stock – *n.* A device that attaches to a semi-automatic weapon to harness recoil and effectively convert a semi-automatic weapon to a machine gun. The term gained national attention in 2017 after bump stock devices enabled a lone gunman allegedly to kill fifty-eight people in Las Vegas. Effective March 2019, bump stock type devices were included in the definition of "machine gun" making them illegal for civilians to possess. Any civilian possessing a bump stock is required to destroy the device or turn it into an ATF office by appointment. (ATF.gov website, 1JAN 2022) Owning a bump stock is punishable by fines and up to ten years in prison. (fox8.com, Fox 8 Cleveland WJW 26 MAR 2019)

carbine – *n.* A light-weight rifle having a short barrel, less than twenty inches. A carbine having a barrel length shorter than sixteen inches is classified by the ATF as a "short barrel rifle" or (SBR). SBRs require a special $200 tax stamp issued by the ATF which may take up to a year to be issued. Even if you shorten the barrel yourself at home it is still considered to be an SBR by the ATF and therefore subject to regulation.

cartridge – A *cartridge* is an assembly of component parts including a casing, a primer, a measured quantity of gunpowder, and a bullet protruding out of the leading end.

casing – The outer cylinder of a round which contains the charging chemicals, the propellant, and which supports the bullet in position for launch.

center fire – *adj. D*escribes a cartridge having the igniter or primer centered in the base. Center fire cartridges require a firearm that strikes the cartridge on center rather than on the rim as in rim fire.

choke – *n.* A device usually threaded inside and at the end of a shotgun barrel, used to control the spray. Shotguns used for sport may be sold with one or more removable chokes that vary the spray effect of the shot.

compensator – *n.* Same as "muzzle break". A device placed on the end of a gun barrel that lessens recoil by releasing some of the back pressure as a bullet flies out of a gun.

direct gas impingement – *adj.* Describes a firearm mechanism that directs some expanding gas from a shot fired into a gas tube creating a reward force, which resets the bolt and firing assembly.

piston gas system – *n.* A firearm mechanism that uses a gas driven piston to reload the next ammo as it ejects the spent shell or cartridge which resets the semi auto action similarly to the Direct Gas Impingement ending result..

double action – A firearm having double action can be operated by cocking the hammer back manually as in a single action gun, or it may be operated by simply pulling the trigger hard enough to set the hammer. It can be fired two ways, hence the descriptor "double action".

double action revolver – *n.* See above.

dry fire – The practice of activating a firearm minus any ammunition.

exposed hammer – A hammer-like component of a pistol or revolver situated at the rear of a firing mechanism. It is exposed and can be set to the cocked position using the thumb, while maintaining a grip using three fingers. The index finger is reserved as the trigger finger. Exposed hammers can be found on rifles, handguns, pistols.

FFL – Stands for Federal Firearms License or Licensee.

flat base – A term used to describe a more or less cone-shaped bullet flattened on the trailing end, as opposed to the "boattail base" shape that tapers to the rear.

flat-nosed bullets – Bullets that are flat on the leading end, these bullets are popular for exhibition; they provide a crisp punch to the target.

frangible – *adj.* Used to describe bullets that thoroughly disintegrate on impact, used effectively for self-defense. These are used for police training in close spaces due to the low likelihood of ricochet. These bullets leave no toxic materials on the field-of-fire environment.

friendly fire – Unintended, confused gunfire in the direction of an ally.

form 4473 – A Federal form completed at the time a firearm is transferred.

GCA – Gun Control Act, legislation passed in 1968 that regulated the purchase of firearms, set up requirements for serial numbers, and added other regulations related to the sale of firearms.

ghost gun – *n. A*n unserialized gun, often sensationalized for emotional effect. These may be the result of 3-D printing, or the assembly of scavenged parts.

ghost ring site – *n. A* circular site, used as the front or rear site on a rifle or shotgun.

green tips – *n. L*ight armor penetrating rounds, usually 62-grain. Containing steel and which are tipped green.

gun lock – *n.* A device used to block the action of a gun, sometimes used when guns are stored.

hollow point – *n. A* bullet having the center core hollowed out. Hollow points expand on impact to a wider tract than the original bullet shape, transferring more energy to the target. Hollow points are better defensively as they are less likely to pass through and hit an unintended target.

hoplophobia – *n. E*xcessive fear of firearms. Hoplo is Greek for weapon.

Kevlar – A high strength synthetic fiber or fabric used in "bullet proof" vests.

lever action – Describes a type of rifle having a manually operated, curved, cocking handle that when racked forward removes any spent cartridge, and with rearward motion it moves the next cartridge into the chamber. Lever action rifles were made famous in numerous TV Westerns and in military operations from the American Civil War through WWI.

loading indicator – An indicator on various firearms that show that the firearm is loaded and ready to fire.

MOA – *n.* Minute of Angle. A concept used in adjusting the angle of fire from a firearm, and/or the angle of a scope to correct down-range accuracy at target. 1 MOA (only 1/60 of a degree) is a tiny measure of correction that results in an ever-widening correction at the target. Changing the angle of fire 1 MOA results in a 1" difference on the target at 100 yds; 2" at 200 yds; 3" at 300 yds; … out to 8" at 800 yds. (NSSF the Firearm Industry Trade Association nssf.org/shooting/minute-angle-moa/ viewed 08 JAN 2022) MOA is used to coordinate the functions of a rifle with a scope. The process is called zeroing.

Magnum – A gun designed to fire cartridges that are more powerful than the caliber would suggest. (Oxford Languages, Google's English dictionary)

moon clip – A flattened metal (rarely plastic) form that holds cartridges for easy loading into a revolver. The moon clip enables firing of ammo normally fired from a semi-automatic.

muzzle – The open end of a gun barrel from which the bullet exits.

musket – A black powder muzzle loaded rifle.

muzzle break – A device that screws on to the end of a barrel to compensate, direct, and disburse the blast for less recoil.

muzzle cap – A dust cover for a muzzle for storage.

muzzle loader – The oldest known true firearm on earth, the muzzle-loading rifle, primitive by today's standards, was fired by igniting black powder behind a bullet inside a barrel. Initially used for sport and hunting, the muzzle-loader rapidly became the choice weapon of war.

muzzle shroud – A cover for a muzzle that extends beyond the tip and helps to direct the sound and the blast. This is a different product from a silencer or suppressor.

NFA – National Firearms Act passed by Congress in 1934 enacted because of Chicago's excessive gang violence, fast-forward to 2023 Chicago still deals with excessive gang violence.

objective lens – One of the lenses of a rifle scope, the one more distant from the ocular lens, and furthest from the eye of the shooter.

ordinance – *n.* Materials and equipment used in warfare, guns, ammo, tanks, rockets, drones, and the like.

out of battery – The phrase means that if/when the slide on a magazine-loaded semi-automatic is out of position, the gun cannot be fired.

parallax – Or parallax error, a visual distortion that may occur with the use of a rifle scope, corrected by adjusting the scope's windage (left to right) and elevation adjustments.

plinking – v. Shooting steel targets usually using inexpensive ammo, often just for fun. A commonly used expression for shooting .22s.

polymer – A hard plastic used for gun frames, popularized by Glock in the '80s. Polymer gun frames were controversial when first introduced as they might defeat airport security at the time. Polymers are also used for hardened gun-specific holsters.

primer – The *primer*, located in the base of the cartridge or shell, receives the impact of the firing pin. The primer consists of a small metal alloy cup containing a minute amount of an explosive chemical that ignites the propellant inside a cartridge.

print or printing – The tell-tale outline of a firearm under clothing. Printing defeats the purpose of concealed carry. Imagine the shape of an FN 503 inside the waistband of biker pants. The outline you see is the "print". You will notice a distinct fashion trend of loose and baggy clothes among those of us who carry concealed.

propellant – The gunpowder; black powder, or nitrocellulose, the "smokeless" substance that ignites to a rapid controlled burn when a unit of ammo is fired.

Puckle gun – An early forerunner of automatic weaponry patent no. 418, Old England in 1718. On a good day with a good crew, it could fire sixty-three bullets in seven minutes.

pump-action – An action most commonly found on shotguns and some rifles in which the fore-end grip, or hand guard, can be manipulated to eject a spent shell, and with forward motion lifts and loads the next unit of ammo.

rack – To engage a slide action to load or eject a cartridge or to show the firearm is free of ammo, or clear.

recoil – The "kick" that the shooter experiences when a gun is fired. This push-back is harnessed in some firearms to eject a spent cartridge and to cycle the next round into position.

red dot site (sometimes green) – A gun site that can be used in addition to iron sites to improve accuracy in rapid fire shooting, an optic that appears to project a red dot on an objective lens using a system of small mirrors aligned right to left and vertical to horizontal. The dot appears only to the person looking through the site.

reticles – Lines that appear in the eyepiece of a gun site to aid aiming. Aka "cross-hairs".

revolver – A firearm, usually a handgun, having a rotating cylinder positioned between the grip and the barrel and directly above the trigger guard, which serves as a carrier to rotate cartridges into the firing position.

ricochet – *v.* To rebound off a hard surface.

rimfire – *adj.* Refers to a cartridge that has the primer located in the rim of the base. Rimfire cartridges require rimfire firearms, in which the firing pin strikes the rim at the base of the cartridge.

RIP ammo – *Radically Invasive Projectile (RIP)*, having trocars that fan out on impact.

round – A general term for a cartridge or shotgun shell.

rubber bullets – Cartridges or shells designed to be less lethal. These may be composed of metal, plastic, or wood, usually with a thin, rubberized outer layer.

select fire – A feature of a firearm that enables the shooter to choose automatic, semi-automatic, or in some cases, multiple round bursts by means of moving a switch or lever.

shot shells – Analogous to cartridges, shot shells contain the materials ignited and expelled when a shotgun is fired.

sidearm – *n.* Usually a holstered pistol.

silencer – The words "silencer" and "suppressor" mean the same thing: a device placed on the muzzle of a firearm for the purpose of sound suppression.

single action – Describes a firearm that requires manual cocking. A trigger pull then results in one shot fired.

single-action revolver – An older design for a revolver that requires a manual cocking of the hammer, and a trigger pull to function. This design allows a smooth trigger pull and a reportedly greater accuracy.

single and/or double action revolver – This is a revolver that can operate in two ways. It may be cocked manually before the trigger pull, or cocking the hammer can happen as result of a two-stage trigger pull, which cocks and fires the gun with one squeeze of the trigger.

sintering – A process of powder metallurgy which presses metal into a compressed powder for use in frangible bullets.

skeet shoot(ing) – A competition sport involving shotguns and rapidly flung clay targets.

snake shot – Ammo that scatters small lead pellets, useful against snakes and small pests.

snap cap – An ammunition substitute, a false cartridge, that fits a firearm in the same way a cartridge fits, used to receive the impact of the firing pin in practice firing. It is free of chemicals and has no bullet. Use of a snap cap allows practice without the problems associated with dry firing.

speed loader – A device used to improve the speed of replacing ammo in a revolver.

sporting clays – A game that involves shooting at moving clay targets using a shotgun.

straw purchase – "Buying a gun for someone who is prohibited by law from possessing one or buying for someone who does not want his or her name associated with the purchase is a 'straw purchase'.

An illegal firearm purchase (straw purchase) is a federal crime."
(dontlie.org, A National Campaign to Prevent the Illegal , viewed
08JAN 2022)

styphnate – An amber-colored crystalline substance, which is a
highly explosive, impact sensitive, chemical, that has molecules
that are loaded with oxygen atoms, enabling it to burn without air!
Styphnate is used as a primer for cartridges.

subsonic ammo – Ammunition that delivers bullets or lugs that
move slower than the speed of sound.

tap-rack-bang – This is a memory aid used to help clear a jammed
cartridge when a semi-auto slide does not go into position due
to a misaligned cartridge or spent casing that failed to eject. The
shooter taps the side or back of the pistol to shake out the cartridge
, then racks the slide, and after the slide goes into the correct position the gun can be fired, bang.

tactical – carefully planned, usually for military purposes.

tracer ammo – *n.* A bullet that streams light, used by the military
to shed light on a field of fire.

target – Any object deliberately fired upon. More generally, a goal.

trap shooting – A type of sport shooting using a shotgun fired at
clay targets which are thrown from an oscillating target thrower.

trigger take up – *n.* That distance the trigger moves prior to initi-
ating the gunfire.

trigger wall – *n.* The final point in movement of a trigger before
the mechanism fires the cartridge.

turkey shoot – *n.* A sport shooting competition usually held around Thanksgiving, where the winner is awarded a turkey.

Twenty-one Gun Salute – A military tradition used to honor fallen heroes. The traditional seven-person three-volley firing of rifles, though commonly referred to as a Twenty-one Gun Salute, is contested by a few purists who believe an official salute must be done with cannons. The origins of the Twenty-one Gun Salute probably began before guns existed, with a throwing down of weapons, swords and such, as a sign of meeting in peace. Early firearms were disabled by firing a single shot, as reloading was a slow process. Thus, firing the weapons into the air was emblematic of a commitment to do no harm. Back in 1730, the British recommended Twenty-one Guns as a salute, as they entered friendly harbors. At the time the US Navy adopted the Twenty-one Gun Salute, the US just happened to have Twenty-one states, so the military tradition was established for America. (Joe Oliveto, What's a 21 Gun Salute for Military Funerals? 1/21/21 www.joincake. com/blog/21-gun-salute/)

twist rate – The rate of spin as a bullet travels outward.

velocity – *n.* The measure of speed.

wad or wads – *n.* A component in a shotgun shell traditionally made of felt, fiber, and/or cork. Due to environmental concerns, there is a return to these materials. Wads were once a separate item used for muzzle loading.

wildcat cartridge – *n.* Custom made cartridges not used for police or military service.

wing shoot – *v.* To shoot birds in flight. Skeet shooting mimics wing shooting.

zeroing – The process of adjusting a scope for shooting accuracy.

MORE GUN-LOADED LANGUAGE

Bullet proof: failsafe, secure.

Cheap shot: Acts or statements that are needless, disrespectful, rude, unsportsmanlike, and uncalled for.

Dead on target: perfectly accurate.

Don't bring a knife to a gun fight: this is a way of saying be prepared to match the opponent's capabilities.

Don't give them ammunition: hold back any information that might be useful to opponent.

Give it the gun: run full power.

Go off half-cocked: an idiom, to start without thinking it through.

Going great guns: vigorously moving along.

Gunning for: similar to hunting for a trophy… as "gunning for" promotion: campaigning for something.

Gun slinger: 1) One who carries a gun and shoots well 2) a vigorous participant in a given sphere (Dictionary Oxford Languages). Reckless, yet capable.

High caliber: 1) High-quality, highly capable. Refers to people as well as to firearms. 2) large bore or large diameter (https://www. lexico.com>definition).

Jumped the gun: acted too hastily. Started the race before the gun was fired. (www.dictionary.com)

Keep your powder dry: means remain cautious and prepared for an opportunity. .

Loaded for bear: ready for a big challenge or confrontation. The literal meaning, loaded with a large enough caliber cartridge to effectively stop big game.

Long shot: a contender that has little or no chance of winning.

More bang for the buck: a phrase that originated in the '60s referring to military spending for firepower (DICTIONARY.COM).

On target: progressing in the right direction at a desirable speed.

Outgunned: out-performed, also, a situation in which the opponent has superior firing capability.

Packing heat: carrying a firearm, usually concealed.

Pull the trigger on: act on a proposition, close a deal, finally decide on a course of action.

Ready, Aim, Fire: a familiar phrase taken from military or firing squad instructions, intended to coordinate the weapon assault.

Ready, Fire, Aim: a phrase taken from firing squad instructions that rearranges the sequence. It means don't get bogged down. Don't overthink. Respond quickly. This mantra has been adopted in corporate workplaces, with mixed results. (Coates, Steve i-lead. com/ila-articles/ready-fire-aim/ viewed 08Jan22)

Riding shotgun: maintaining a supportive look-out position during transport. To look out for threats to a mission or to another person.

Shoot the breeze: engage in aimless relaxed pleasant conversation.

Shoot the bull: engage in entertaining conversation which is otherwise pointless and questionable.

Shot in the dark: an effort made with little hope for a successful outcome.

Shoot oneself in the foot: to unintentionally interfere with one's own case or effort.

Shot me down: rejected, foiled, or disappointed, or refused.

Sitting duck: from duck hunting, a person or thing that is easy prey.

So shoot me: a phrase of admission of wrong thinking or behavior that conveys an expectation of overreaction to the error.

Stick to your guns: originally, this referred to a gunner remaining by his post. The current meaning is that one should tenaciously stay with an opinion, statement or course of action. (www.dictionary.com, viewed 30 October 2021)

Hold your fire: stop arguing.

Take a shot at: to give something a try.

ABOUT THE AUTHOR

GABRIEL KARR LIVES IN NORTH CAROLINA. He served his country as a Navy Corpsman for more than a decade. He has worked in the firearms industry for more than ten years in retail gun sales. He's frequently the top salesperson at his work place.

He is a strong supporter of all things constitutional, particularly the Second Amendment. His interest in firearms goes well back to his childhood. As a kid approaching his twelfth birthday, he ran an optimistic, but failed, campaign for a birthday gift of a .454 Casull Revolver, the only item on his wish list. At the age of twelve, he simply couldn't fathom why it was denied. To him, it was an obvious necessity.

He enjoys hiking the many trails in the North Carolina State Parks and kayaking with friends. After a day on the river, Gabriel loves grilling in his backyard with pals, especially on Independence Day. He is a great spontaneous cook and loves concocting special marinades. His secret is bacon drippings on everything! He is fond of growing jalapeno peppers because they have "ten times the vitamin C of oranges." He uses lots of them in his marinades.

He believes responsible firearm ownership contributes to fewer unwanted incidents, less crime, and an overall better quality of life for everyone. He loves sharing his firearm knowledge. Based on his observations of thousands of people and their firearms, he has assembled this work as a guide for appreciating the finer points of firearm ownership, as he sees it, the mark of a free people.

www.ingramcontent.com/pod-product-compliance
Lightning Source LLC
Chambersburg PA
CBHW061426160726

47995CB00003B/769